WHO AUTHORED THE JOHN TITOR LEGEND?

MIKE SAUVE

Although the author and publisher have made every effort to ensure that the information in this book was correct at press time, the author and publisher do not assume and hereby disclaim any liability to any party for any loss, damage, or disruption caused by errors or omissions, whether such errors or omissions result from negligence, accident, or any other cause.

Copyright © 2016

Mike Sauve

The author wishes to thank Dan Scott, Larry Haber, Joseph Matheny, Temporal Recon, Wayne E. Pederson, Dave Scott and Jeff Newman for their help in the researching and writing of this book.

CONTENTS

Introduction	1
The John Titor Story	9
The Suspects	25
Larry Haber	27
An Interview with Larry Haber	35
Richard and Morey Haber	39
Joseph Matheny	45
An Interview with Joseph Matheny	57
Temporal Recon	67
An Interview with Temporal Recon	83
Oliver Williams	89
The Bit Players	95
Pre-Existing Influences	97
Art Bell	107
Pamela	117
Hoax Hunter	121
Steven Gibbs	123
Marlin Pohlman	129
Conclusion	137

INTRODUCTION

It was way too late at night and I was on the weird part of YouTube again. I found myself listening to an old Art Bell *Coast to Coast* episode on time travel. Everyone's been down these rabbit holes. But the one I went down was exceptionally deep. In fact I'm still descending into it to this day. Because one clip led to another, and before the night was through I was listening to Art's *Coast to Coast* successor George Noory discussing the time traveler John Titor. I Googled as I listened. Who was John Titor? How did he make the accurate predictions he did? Were those pull-out drawings of a time machine as legitimate as they first appeared? Wanting answers to these questions, I began reading the hundreds of pages of online posts left by John Titor.

Much like Art Bell, and presumably you, the reader interested enough to purchase this book, I have always loved time travel. Recently I completed a work of fiction called *I Ain't Got No Home In This World Anymore* in which the narrator goes back to alternate world lines and deals with similar-but-different versions of himself, along with all the concomitant ego dysfunction, obnoxiousness, and dilettantism anyone might find in their sixteen-year-old self. Like Professor Ronald Mallet, whose interest in building a time machine stemmed from a desire to interact with his deceased father, I am fixated on my own past.

And yet my primary motivation is not to prove that John Titor was a real time traveler, but rather to look at the possible authors of the John Titor story. By no means is my intention to viciously debunk the John Titor story so that skeptics can point blindly to this book and say something like, "John Titor was a sham. Kill yourself," as one 4chan /x/ poster responded to a John Titor thread recently.

Instead, I hope the book might even serve to debunk skeptics who dismiss the case as being simplistic and unworthy of serious scrutiny. They take a minute or two, note that John Titor predicted civil war in 2004, or that there'd be no Olympics after that same year, and case closed, another obnoxious splinter group that won't worship at the big grey altar of logic can be snidely castigated.

If John Titor is a time traveler, then that's the most exciting thing to happen in my lifetime. No one would be happier to see conclusive proof than me. But assuming he is not, then the question of who developed this story, how they were able to make the accurate predictions they did, why their identity/identities have remained secret for so long, and why occasional tidbits of information continue to leak out even fifteen years later, well, all that makes for one hell of a mystery.

I will make the case against six people who may be behind the John Titor legend, either independently or in conjunction. I use the term *legend* rather than *hoax* because of the negative connotation associated with *hoaxers*, and also because *legend* is the most fitting term to describe the John Titor phenomenon.

University of California folklore and mythology professor Robert Georges defines a legend as, "A story or narrative that may not be a story or narrative at all; it is set in a recent history or historical past that may be conceived to be remote or antihistorical or not really past at all; it is believed to be true by some, false by others, or both or neither by most."

Just switch that part about *history* with *the future* and it applies perfectly to the writings of John Titor. A hoaxer, on the other hand, is typically looking for personal gain, or to make someone else look foolish. It's not known whether the author(s) of the John Titor story aspired to financial gain. Surely they haven't achieved any.

Among the primary suspects are Larry Haber: an entertainment lawyer who operates the John Titor Foundation Limited Liability Corporation, claims to represent John Titor's mother 'Kay Titor,' and who was responsible for the publication of *John Titor: A Time Traveler's Tale*.

Haber's brothers, Morey and Richard Haber: who have faced accusation from both The Hoax Hunter and (in Richard's case) a private investigator hired by the Italian television program *Voyager*.

Joseph Matheny: an innovator in the world of alternate reality gaming who has claimed to be one of four authors behind the Titor story.

Oliver Williams: the webmaster behind JohnTitor.com who has become a de facto spokesperson for the story.

And Temporal Recon: author of *Conviction of a Time Traveler,* a self-published book that makes a lawyerly case that John Titor was indeed a real time traveler.

Other bit-players who are not suspected of creating the John Titor legend, but who did factor into the story in some way will also be discussed.

These include The Hoax Hunter: a peerless Internet troll and surprisingly effective detective.

Marlin Pohlman: a PhD who submitted a patent application for a time machine based entirely on schematics provided in the John Titor posts.

And Pamela Moore: the poster who bonded with John over instant messaging chats, and claims to possess evidence that uniquely qualifies her to disqualify any fakes coming forward as John Titor.

Much of the best evidence is buried at the 1 hour 47 minute mark of old radio interviews, just as most of the best Titor speculation has taken place on message boards like *Above Top Secret, Paranormalis,* and similar sites, so I've drawn from those sources. At the very least, I hope this book can serve as a helpful reference for fellow Titor devotees. It's not my intention to 'convict' any suspected author(s), but rather to present all the best evidence in an impartial manner.

I am assuming the reader of this book has a basic level of knowledge regarding the John Titor story. If not, this introduction is followed by what I considered the most interesting details. It's advised that new initiates begin by reading the complete John Titor posts. They are widely available on the Internet, but a supplementary PDF is also available for download at www.mikesauve.com

For a brief introduction to the 'chronology' of John's story, I refer readers to this useful timeline created by an anonymous 4chan poster (overleaf).

Who Authored the John Titor Legend?

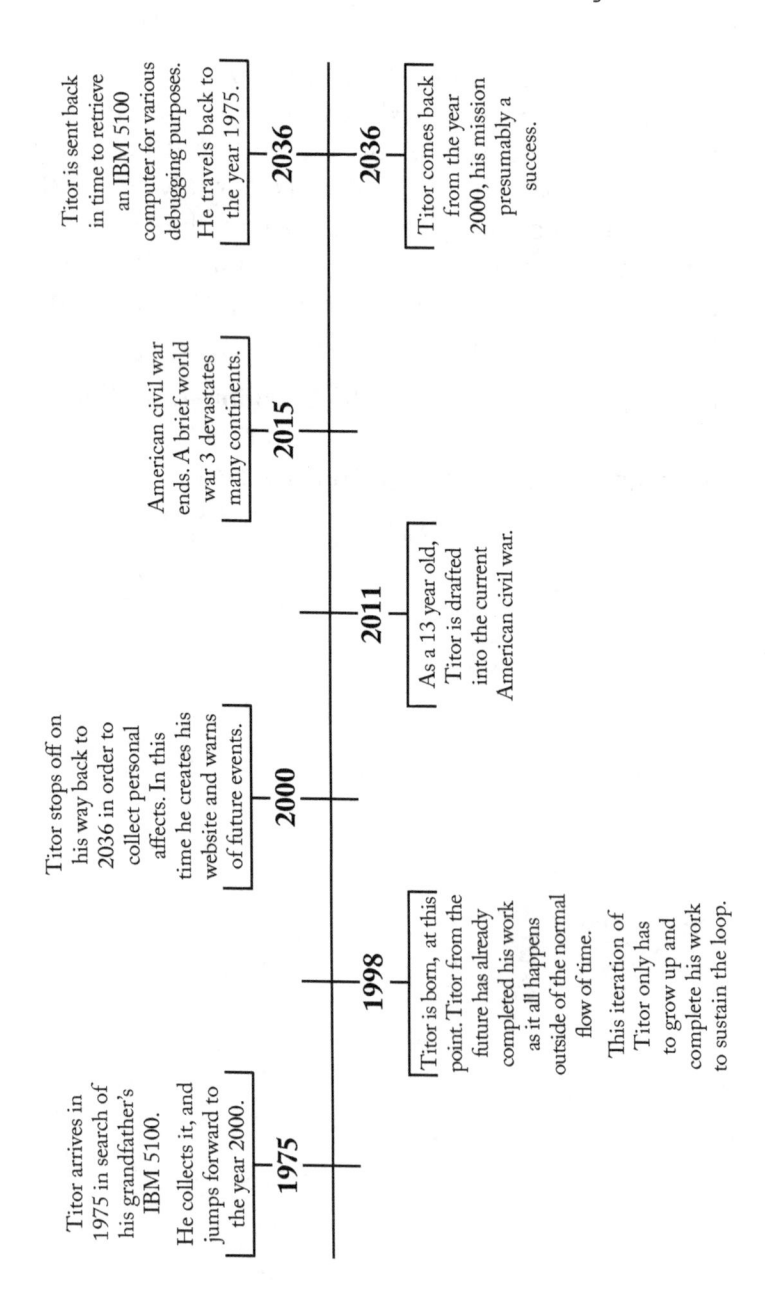

1975 — Titor arrives in 1975 in search of his grandfather's IBM 5100. He collects it, and jumps forward to the year 2000.

1998 — Titor is born, at this point. Titor from the future has already completed his work as it all happens outside of the normal flow of time. This iteration of Titor only has to grow up and complete his work to sustain the loop.

2000 — Titor stops off on his way back to 2036 in order to collect personal affects. In this time he creates his website and warns of future events.

2011 — As a 13 year old, Titor is drafted into the current American civil war.

2015 — American civil war ends. A brief world war 3 devastates many continents.

2036 — Titor is sent back in time to retrieve an IBM 5100 computer for various debugging purposes. He travels back to the year 1975.

2036 — Titor comes back from the year 2000, his mission presumably a success.

THE JOHN TITOR STORY

On January 27, 2001 a man calling himself John Titor posted this on Art Bell's *Post to Post* message board.

> Greetings. I am a time traveler from the year 2036. I am on my way home after getting an IBM 5100 computer system from the year 1975.
>
> My "time" machine is a stationary mass, temporal displacement unit manufactured by General Electric. The unit is powered by two, top-spin, dual-positive singularities that produce a standard, off-set Tipler sinusoid.
>
> I will be happy to post pictures of the unit.

The Internet was a much different place in 2001 than it is today. We're currently enjoying/suffering through what's called Web 2.0. We spend the majority of our time on social media rather than individual websites, are connected to the Internet 24/7, and trolling has blossomed from being an occasional nuisance to a thriving sub-culture.

There were, simply put, less cranks and role players online in 2001. John Titor distinguished himself as a non-crank and, at the very least, a talented role-player with a surprising depth of detail to his story, not to mention an apparent maturity and sophistication.

> **Posted by John Titor on 01-28-2001 06:35 AM**
>
> Also, I realize there is no way for anyone to believe me with absolute certainty so I hope I'm at least entertaining. You may be interested to know that even in 2036, there are a large number of people who don't believe in time travel. Are you sure the world is round?

At the turn of the millennium, many people were still connecting via dial-up, and going online for a half hour to an hour a day. So the *Post to Post* or the *Time Travel Institute* board members actually had something of themselves invested. They weren't just listlessly scrolling through their phones while waiting in lines or sitting on mass transit. Think of them more like attendees at a conference than the basement dwellers you'd find today on Reddit or BellGab. While many were sceptical, an overall tone of respect characterizes most of their addresses to John. There's a refreshing lack of the snarky responses that would greet a story as incredible as John Titor's today.

Posters asked intelligent questions about the physics and the philosophy of time travel, as well as the sociological conditions of the future. What makes the John Titor story so rich is that without fail John gives thoughtful and largely credible responses to each of these queries. In the chat room discussions John participated in, he was equally capable of answering in real time. The only aspect of John's discourse that suffers when he's under pressure for a quick response is his spelling.

>TimeTravel_0 : I enjoy the "paranormal" chat rooms for 2 reasons.

>TimeTravel_0 : 1. I find the people here are more open to ideas.

>TimeTravel_0 : 2. I find it ironic that when what they are looking for falls in their lap, they can't believe it.

It's worth considering these mediums that John Titor used because just as the John Titor legend is about a time traveler on the Internet, it is also a legend about the Internet itself.

As folklorist Michael Kinsella writes, "It makes perfect sense that legends have arisen about the Internet, for this is a medium in which the imagination, intuition, and fuzzy logic reign; ideas surrounding instantaneous global communication exhibit many supernatural themes, and cyberspace allows people to externalize or evince their imaginings in an environment where fact and fiction become intermingled with beliefs and hoaxes.

In a very real sense, the Internet is a province for mysteries and the supernatural, and as such, legends about it flourish."

John claims he was initially sent from the year 2036 to the year 1975. His mission was to retrieve an IBM 5100. Because of its unique capability to emulate programs from both the BASIC and APL programming languages, this computer would help prevent a UNIX timeout in the year 2038. Here was the first bit of credibility that would emerge only later. It turns out the 5100 did have this unique capability. And only a select few involved in the engineering of the 5100 knew about this at the time of the Titor posts. John said he was chosen for the mission because he was related to one of the IBM 5100 engineers. The identity of this engineer has become its own cottage industry of speculation.

From 1975 John returns to 2000 on a personal mission, but also to archive information to be brought back to 2036. Some of this archival research involved his message board interactions. During this time he lived with his parents and even his infant self.

Posted by Charlotte Boren on 02-06-2001 07:11 AM

Is it possible for you to bump into yourself when you are time travelling? Saw a Jean Claude Van Dam movie about that once. I think it was called "Time Cop". Whatever you do, don't shake hands with yourself, if you do meet.

Posted by John Titor on 02-06-2001 08:33 AM

Yes that is possible and there are no limitations on interacting with them. I find it interesting that there is some sort of collective negativity with the idea of doing that. Could it be that we are not really that comfortable with ourselves and therefore we cannot imagine meeting, liking or helping another one of us on another world line?

John said that Waco-type sieges would begin occurring on a monthly basis, precipitating a United States civil war in 2004 that would pit rural areas against metropolitan ones. Soon after, major U.S. cities of the "American Federal Empire" would be nuked by Russia. Living in rural Florida, John and his family would have considered the cities and the AFE their enemy; still, every American's life changes after "N Day."

John then weaves a rich tale of his adolescence in post-nuclear America. He describes a political system that involves five regional presidents. Omaha, Nebraska becomes the U.S. capital. People are forced to rely on their neighbours, and are mistrustful of any food that they can't trace the origins of. As a 13-year-old, John fought as a member of a shotgun infantry called the Fighting Diamondbacks.

Knowing the constitution, practising self-sustainability and the importance of family are among the major themes in the John Titor posts. He also castigates his 'contemporary' interlocutors on a number of fronts, including their interest in vapid subjects like sporting events, their lack of concern over mad cow disease, and their false sense of security.

Of course, no U.S. civil war occurred in 2004, and America remains, as yet, un-nuked. Believers point to John's statement that our world line has a 2.5% divergence from his own, which means nothing that happened on his world line was guaranteed to happen on ours. For sceptics this represents too easy of an out, placing John's story in the loathsome category of "unfalsifiable," leading many to dismiss the story out of hand the moment they come across what Wikipedia lists as John's "predictive failures."

Another aspect that makes the John Titor posts unfalsifiable is that time and again John refused to make predictions that would allow anyone to benefit financially, avoid death by probability, or change their future.

Posted by John Titor on 02-02-2001 10:09 AM

I could probably find some way to even charge you for it. When the day comes for my "prediction" to be realized it will either happen or not. If it does happen, then your ability to judge your environment is crippled by your acceptance of me as a "knower of all things" and gifted with the ability to tell the future. If I am wrong, then everything I have said that might possibly have made you think about your world in a different way is suddenly discredited. I do not want either. Although I do have personal reasons for being here and speaking with you, the most I could hope for is that you recognize the possibility of time travel as a reality. You are able to change your world line for better or worse just as I am.[...] Therefore, any "prediction" I might make has a slight chance of being incorrect anyway and you now have the ability to act on it based on what I've said. Can you stop the war before it gets here? Sure. Will you do it? Probably not.

These factors are ideal for the skeptic, who doesn't want to devote a lot of time to his debunking. But before the John Titor story can be dismissed so easily we must look at all the things John Titor predicted correctly.

If John Titor was not a time traveller, then he had access to a broad range of rarified information spanning several fields of study, knew a great deal about contemporary physics and CERN, and possessed a writer's ability to craft a compelling narrative. He also produced a pull-out drawing (see below) of his C204 Gravity Distortion Time Displacement Unit that would have taken a professional draftsman up to a full work week to produce, according to some estimates.

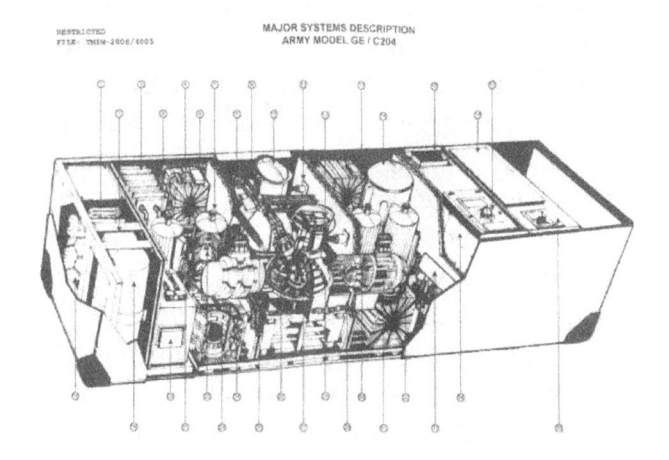

For me, this mix of talents combined with the persevering mystery of who's behind the posts, is even more fascinating than the "is John Titor a real time traveller?" question.

My favourite correct prediction is perhaps the most mundane. In 2001 a large marketing campaign advertised the mysterious Project Ginger. A poster asked John to identify what this project would yield. Presumably the only people who knew what Project Ginger was were the creator's team and those entrusted with marketing and distribution.

Posted by Mike Kolesnik on 01-29-2001 06:38 PM

What is the "Ginger" (IT) invention?

Posted by John Titor on 01-29-2001 09:10 PM

It looks like some sort of motorized scooter. What do you think "IT" is?

Project Ginger, as we now know, would eventually yield the Segway.

It's not impossible that one of the John Titor authors had access to this information, but what are the odds that someone would ask this very question? The only way it's probable is if the questioners themselves were plants. This is a theory the self-styled Hoax Hunter has put forth with some validity, asserting that the majority of posters interacting with John have very little Internet presence outside of these message boards.

John also foresaw many technological changes that would have been difficult to predict in 2001. When asked to describe the Internet of 2036, he says:

Posted by John Titor on 02-10-2001 09:49 AM

Actually, you will probably be quite impressed with our internet. It's based on a series of independent, self-powered nodes that are mobile and can be put up anywhere. It looks a great deal like your current cell phone system.

When asked about the entertainment industry:

> **Posted by John Titor on 02-09-2001 02:02 PM**
>
> Yes, there is an entertainment industry. Again, it is very decentralized. The technology to express yourself with video is so readily available that many people do it all by themselves or in small groups. Much of the distribution is over the web. I would compare it theater here.

This sounds a lot like YouTube, a site that wouldn't become popular until 2006. There's another bit in that quote that stands out for me. It's the word *web*. Not many people call the Internet *the web* in 2016. I guess that too would be chalked up to divergence. In John Titor's world line, I guess calling the Internet *the web* never went out of fashion.

At one point John says that his countrymen are inspired by a poem called *A Soldier's Winter*. No such poem existed in 2001, but according to FamilyFriendPoems.com, who published *A Soldier's Winter* in 2011, after it had been written and self-published in 2005 by a retired U.S. Colonel at the Department of Defence named Larry Cluck, it is:

> Based on a soldier's letter to his daughter.

After the atrocities witnessed at several places in Hiroshima, Vietnam, Iraq, it is warning to the future not to allow the current world to continue in its manner.

I'd be willing to chalk this up to coincidence. *A Soldier's Winter* isn't so unlikely a title after all. But just read it and compare it to John's statements:

A Soldier's Winter
By Larry Cluck

The day before it wasn't snowing.
After amber suns made our Earth now glowing.

The trees are strangers, leering, disapproving
In the ash of winter, our minds are now moving

My world, my life, my wandering path.
It seems not God, but man's own wrath.

I pray God's eyes may see us once again,
Gaze upon us at our end.

We will rebuild, we will renew,
From a world of greed and lust that left so few.

Remind me that I am still his child.
And provide us with your mercy mild.

When asked if he remembered any poetry written after 2001, here are John Titor's exact words:

Posted by John Titor on 02-21-2001 08:48 PM

A Soldier's Winter

The day before it wasn't snowing.
The trees are strangers, leering, disapproving in the ash of winter

..my world, my life, my wandering path. I pray God's eyes may once again gaze upon me and remind me that I am still His child.

I only (think) I remember the first line but the last one I remember. It has quite a few more lines that I don't remember. It is rumored this was written first as a letter by a soldier. After he died it was added to and edited by others. In my opinion, it has become a symbol for the collective guilt my parents' generation feels for what became of the world.

The *My World, My Life, my wandering path* line is exact. Other lines are similar but not exact, which would lend credence to the idea of John trying to remember a poem without being able to Google it.

If John isn't a time traveler, then we have to assume there either was no soldier, and this was planted by the authors of the John Titor story. Or, less probably, the soldier who wrote this exceptional poem plagiarized John Titor for kicks. The author Larry Cluck does appear to be a legitimate U.S. veteran and he claims to have no knowledge of John Titor. When contacted by Oliver Williams, Cluck was bemused by the whole phenomenon, but asserted that the poem was written by him with no help from any time traveler.

There are two other *A Soldier's Winter* poems that seem to be more obvious odes/ripoffs of Titor. On the surface the presence of not one but three *A Soldier's Winter* poems might invalidate John's prediction. But it only makes sense that at some point a John Titor enthusiast or two would come forward to make their own *A Soldier's Winter*.

John's final post was in March of 2001. After that the online enthusiasm grew slowly but steadily, thanks in large part to Oliver Williams' website. It's never entirely reached the mainstream, but radio programs like *Coast to Coast AM* and publications like *i09* continue to fan the flames. Just type the words John Titor into a YouTube search, but only if you've got a couple dozen hours to spare.

As mentioned, the John Titor story is frequently dismissed out of hand. If it comes up in conspiratorial or Fortean circles, people seem bored by it, pointing out that the story has been long since debunked. But even if the predictive failures are enough to prove the story untrue, the question of who wrote the posts and why remains far less cut and dry.

For this reason the John Titor story continues to keep aficionados enthralled, with a small but thriving sub-culture that continues to hash out his remarks on various forums and Facebook groups. Most leave their Titor studies for a while and then return to them when there's some minor advance in the story. Like when our first suspect released a new message from John in 2009.

THE SUSPECTS

Larry Haber

"All roads lead to Larry Haber."

– Dan Scott, Admin of the John Titor: The Physics Behind Time Travel Facebook group

Larry Haber is an entertainment lawyer based out of Orlando, Florida. In 2004 he emerged as the lawyer for the pseudonymous (and possibly fictitious) Kay Titor, putative mother to John. He's also the CEO of The John Titor Foundation Limited Liability Corporation. This LLC holds the copyright on Titor's 177th Military Unit insignia (see below). It operates the John Titor Foundation website. And it published *John Titor: A Time Traveler's Tale*, which is nothing more than a collection of the John Titor posts. Now out of print, this book is sold for up to $890 on Amazon. Recently, Haber optioned the John Titor film rights to a third-party filmmaker named Michael Coonce. Before that, Haber was involved in securing rights and clearances for the production of a John Titor film at the family's behest.

"All I can tell you about the film is they spent a bunch of money. I did a lot of paperwork. They got clearances, we did all sorts of stuff to make sure the film was accurate, and then when I thought it was going to get released they decided not to release it. The family—that's it. It's sitting. They say they're going to release it. I have no idea when how, or anything else," said Haber in a radio interview.

Haber claims to have repeatedly asked Kay to come forward, but that she always says "It's not the time." In one *Coast to Coast* interview he acts as a go-between between George Noory and Kay, relaying the questions and then paraphrasing her responses. In *Where is John Titor* Episode 6, an interview with two amateur YouTube sleuths, immediately after stating that he's met Kay personally, Haber makes statements that he later asks to be redacted.

Haber has stated time and again that 'Kay Titor' is just one client who doesn't result in a lot of billable hours. In the scope of his day-to-day practise he's provided legal services for large corporations like Walt Disney Attractions and Universal Studios Florida. By no means is Larry Haber staking his entire claim on the John Titor story.

Sometimes in the alternative media, a person's status as a lawyer is all that's needed to give them lifelong credibility. See, for example, Andrew Basiago. He's a self-proclaimed time traveler who by any measured account is either a con-man or totally insane. He claims to have travelled to Mars, that he's in line to become the next President, is pals with Obama, and etc. This is a man who has passed the bar, and also a man that shouldn't be taken seriously.

Haber is different. He projects that the Titor story is some weird anomaly that fell into his lap, and that it's the last thing in the world he would have created or sought out. He's certainly not out on lucrative speaking tours like Basiago. He has claimed to be, "Baffled, perplexed and everything in between. I have no idea if any of this is real or not or true or not. I know that they [the family] believe it's real."

However, it's not entirely fair to say he wants to distance himself from the story. If he did, he wouldn't continue to make occasional radio appearances to fan the flames. The most consistent head-scratcher of the Titor story applies best to Haber: if he's trying to profit from this fantastic tale, where are the profits? Oliver Williams once joked that if profit is Haber's goal, "He must be the worst entertainment lawyer in the world."

When he has appeared on *Coast to Coast AM* and *Fade to Black with Jimmy Church* to discuss the story, he never conveys much enthusiasm. The best descriptor of Haber's relationship to the story, or at least of what he *projects* as his relationship to the story, would be *bemused*. But during the *Where is John Titor* interview he doesn't seem so much bemused as angry and annoyed, as he's trying to deflect attention from his son Brandon (according to Oliver Williams: Brandon has received death threats from Titor obsessives) and his brother Richard Haber, both of whom appear in the interview, crammed onto a small sofa beside Larry.

Ostensibly, Haber doesn't seem to be hiding anything. He'll accept friend requests from Titor fans. He's a member of the *John Titor: The Physics Behind Time Travel* group on Facebook and will field the occasional query, albeit with short, affirmative/negative type answers. He is my friend on Facebook and based on his content he appears to lead a fairly quotidian life, in which he values family and friends, travel, and live theatre. It definitely doesn't seem like he's meeting up on the regular with nefarious time travelers or CIA psy-ops agents to perpetrate a John Titor hoax.

Joseph Matheny, who will be discussed in detail later, claims to have once threatened Haber to remove the *John Titor: A Time Traveler's Tale* book from Amazon, and that it was removed shortly thereafter. Haber has denied this claim, calling it "bogus." Still, despite the harsh words spoken by Matheny, Counsellor Haber hasn't undertaken any actions against Matheny for slander or defamation of character.

On November 19, 2009, 'Kay Titor' allegedly instructed Haber to post the following content on YouTube, read by an automated voice. The title is *John Titor Letter 177: tempus edax rerum*, which is Latin for *time that devours all things*.

Greetings.

I am the man you know as John Titor. Correction, I am one of the men you know as John. In 1999, I was the second to arrive on the same world line as the other man you know as John.

It was I who wrote the posts in November and January. When I return to 2001, I will write for the final time in March. My mother will release this message to you in November of 2009. The other John wrote the posts in December and February. He, too, will write his final posts in March of 2001.

As I write this now, the date is March 22, 2009 and the divergence is 1.941. This is not the first time I have been in your future. I was here before writing the first posts in 2001. I tried to warn you. I tried to wake you.

As time passes, I fear you will witness the transition from your apathy and dependence, to your children's fall into bondage. I feel sorry for you.

You will not know the peace and freedom I will have when I return home. In spite of my efforts, the war that gave that gift to me may come to you much later. To prove to you who I am, a friend will corroborate the significance of the musical group, the B-52s.

I am sorry about the strife and difficulty you have had these past years. It was required.

As I said, after 1975, when I arrived in 1999, there was already another John there. The two of us devised a plan to return to separate world lines. The plan required that each of us travel to different time periods between 1998 and 2009, and take measurements with our displacement machine.

We had to find a way to communicate these measurements in a way that would last, and could be easily found later. Our first attempt was with the FAX to Art Bell. I traveled to 1998 first, and left the first FAX with Art. The other John traveled there later and was able to find my FAX. He then left the second FAX.

As the plan is now progressing, we were able to use the Internet. The posts we made, and will make, are a foundation we will need to get home. In each month we will post the measurements we had made in various time periods on different world lines.

Every time someone posts about John Titor after 2001, they will become more permanent and easier for me, or another John to find.

If the other John, or even another John ever arrives in your future trying to get home, he will now see the numbers he needs in the posts. If he were to hear this message, he will know what to do. The final measurements are on the website my mother's attorney has overseen.

This is the reason we made the posts. With your help, they will last. They are a sign post to other Johns who are lost, and need our work to return home. For this, I must thank all of you.

One Seven Seven Tempus Edax Rerum Time will devour all things.

At the same time this table was posted to the John Titor Foundation website. It is the only content on the website and remains so to this day. Titor truthers feel it's a grid or mapping device that John Titor or multiple John Titors will require to return to their original world line(s).

John-1

1999DEC28	2.480	
2009MAR12	1.900	
2000OCT12	2.005	NOV POSTS
1998OCT12	2.500	
2001JAN02	2.004	JAN POSTS
2009MAR21	1.941	

John-2

1999DEC28	2.490	
1998JUL29	2.500	
2000NOV27	2.004	DEC POSTS
2009JUL29	1.941	
2001JAN31	2.004	FEB POSTS
1998OCT29	2.500	

In addition to this table, the biggest development Larry might unleash on John Titor fans remains, as yet, under wraps.

"There's also a departure video of John leaving in 2001," Larry told Jimmy Church, "I can't talk much about it. I know people want to see that to make sure John was real. I've seen it once. It looks real to me. I've seen two minutes of it."

A popular theory is that Haber is the front man for whatever consortium is behind the John Titor story. In many people's estimation, including the investigators for the Italian program *Voyager*, this consortium most likely involves Haber's brother Richard Haber, better known to the Internet as John Rick Haber.

An Interview with Larry Haber

Mike Sauve: The November 19, 2009 YouTube message that begins, "Greetings, I am the man you know as John Titor..." fascinates me. Can you take me through the process of Kay delivering this to you? Can you explain why she decided to have her lawyer upload content to YouTube rather than some other third party?

Larry Haber: I was asked to upload the video, and I did. I received the video and the request by email.

Mike Sauve: Similarly, can you describe the logistics around the John Titor Foundation website. Is it funded in perpetuity, or for a certain number of years? Is there any reason to think it may ever be updated?

Larry Haber: I'm not aware of any plans to update it, but that doesn't mean it won't happen. It was set up to facilitate getting information out to the internet. It's not being used for anything else.

Mike Sauve: Now that your son Brandon is working in the aeronautics industry there's increasing speculation that he's behind the story. But by my estimation he would have been fourteen or fifteen when the posts were written. Even for a gifted young man, his authorship of the story at such a young age strikes me as improbable. Can you confirm that an early adolescent Brandon wasn't behind the John Titor posts?

Larry Haber: He was not. But he sure gets a kick out of the posts online that think he is!

Mike Sauve: You've made it clear time and again that the John Titor story isn't a big part of your life or your practise, but rather it's an intriguing diversion that pops up now and again for you. Some people, including Oliver Williams, are curious why you'd then go on programs like *Fade to Black with Jimmy Church* or *Coast to Coast AM* to fan the flames. Can you discuss your motivation behind these appearances?

Larry Haber: It's fun to do. Kay is aware of it and has never asked me to stop.

Mike Sauve: Why is *John Titor: A Time Traveler's Tale* no longer in print?

Larry Haber: Not my decision. But I have never gotten an answer as to why it isn't reprinted, because I have asked many times.

Mike Sauve: Is there still a John Titor film in the works that has been endorsed by the family? Can you detail what happened during past production efforts? There doesn't seem to be much information available. I know the filmmaker Michael Coonce is pitching a feature length project called *Traveler 0, A Time Traveler's Tale*, and that he optioned *A Time Traveler's Tale* from you, but that you otherwise aren't involved. I'm no copyright expert, but since the posts themselves were freely available online I'm not sure why he'd need to option this content.

Larry Haber: No one really needs to option anything, since the info, as you said, is basically all online. I think people ask to do so to get a leg up on any additional info they can get from me. Once in a while, I am able to help out in this regard.

Mike Sauve: As I've mentioned, Joseph Matheny claims he is one of the authors of the John Titor posts, and that he threatened you to remove *A Time Traveler's Tale* from Amazon. When I asked him about this he responded with the italicized content below. It's not very pleasant, but I thought I should give you the opportunity to respond if you are so inclined:

A) John Titor was not a real person.

B) An entertainment attorney put out a book about a fictional person claiming to have received the content from the family of said FICTIONAL PERSON and passed it off as real.

C) What gain? I don't know. MONEY? He saw an exploitable market and one he thought he could exploit without fear of reprisal ("they can't speak up without blowing their cover.") and he was almost right. Your attitude towards this tells me you haven't really dealt with the marginality of the entertainment industry. Compound that already distasteful milieu with the equally grotesquery of the attorney cadre and you have what Gary Busey calls a GUT MAGGOT.

Larry Haber: I've been called a lot of things, but not a maggot so far. His claims are bogus, but I'm not here to argue with anybody.

Mike Sauve: Do you believe Kay's story, and ipso facto, the claims made in the John Titor posts? Or do you think it's possible that there are authors of the John Titor story who have used or employed Kay, and by association the colleague of yours who recommended you, to provide themselves with a layer of removal. If so, whoever's behind this has a budget.

Larry Haber: I've repeatedly stated publicly I have no idea whether any of this is real or not. And I still don't. If it is a group behind this with just an agenda, they've done a very good job of it.

Mike Sauve: Do you spend much time thinking about the consequences of the John Titor story if it is true?

Larry Haber: Nope. It's interesting to me, and fun to participate in. If true, there are too many timelines to juggle to ever get a handle on what is real. So, I don't dwell on it.

Richard and Morey Haber

"What strange creatures brothers are!"

– Jane Austen

Mike Lynch, a private investigator who investigated the John Titor story for the Italian television program *Voyager*, suspected that Richard Haber, known to Lynch then as John "Rick" Haber, was responsible for the John Titor story. As a result, nearly every serious article about John Titor implicates John "Rick" Haber, brother to Larry Haber, ESQ.

Except Larry Haber doesn't have a brother named John "Rick" Haber. Only a brother named Richard Haber.

For both Richard and another Haber brother, Morey Haber, who is the VP of Technology at the cyber security firm Beyond Trust, these accusations have led to some consternation. So much so that Richard participated with his brother Larry in the *Where is John Titor* YouTube interview along with Brandon Haber. Prior to the interview, Larry states that he's interested in using the YouTube investigators' platform for clearing his brother's name, as it was becoming a minor professional problem for Richard.

"My brother was visiting a year ago when I did an interview for Italian television and all of a sudden they thought he was John Titor," Larry Haber told the interviewers, "My brother is an I.T. administrator, so I can see some people having some type of connection. But they [Richard and Brandon] are not John Titor and quite frankly they're getting way too many emails."

As The Hoax Hunter discovered in 2009, the P.O. box (47071) for the John Titor Foundation, then registered to Larry Haber, was previously registered to John R. Haber.

Larry denies Richard's association with the P.O. box, saying, "It's amazing to me that people could get focussed on the red herring of red herrings as we say in the law business. I had a P.O. box in Celebration, downtown Celebration, which is separate from Kissimmee. When I moved out of Celebration I didn't have that P.O. box anymore. How somebody related someone in Kissimmee whose last name was Haber to a box in Kissimmee at an address that doesn't even exist, and never even got to the box in Celebration, which is where it really was is beyond me, and how it became a huge piece of the work on the Internet, no clue. It has nothing to do with anything. I had a P.O. box because I lived here and I worked here. People have shot video over here. I'm not sure why they shot video of those offices."

Larry also denies ever having had a P.O. box under the name of John R. Haber, and says there's no John Haber in the family. "My brother's name is Richard. He's never been known as Rick. Just Richard."

When I asked Larry why the *Voyager* investigator referred to Richard as John Rick, and why P.O. box 47071 was initially registered to John R. Haber, Larry Haber responded in a similar fashion, "I have no idea where John Rick came from. My brother's full name is Richard Scott Haber. The P.O. Box story is totally bogus, as far as I know."

Richard's background in information technology and the fact that Richard happened to be hanging around during the *Voyager* investigation were enough for Mike Lynch to conclude that he was the prime suspect even without the benefit of the P.O. box information.

Richard denies culpability in the *Where is John Titor* interview, saying he has, "Absolutely nothing to do with it. As a matter of fact I didn't even know who John Titor was until I went to [...] take your brother to work day when I happened to come down to his fiftieth birthday party and happened to come down...[to the taping of the *Voyager* interview]."

In addition to his impressive detective work involving the P.O box, The Hoax Hunter later produced a mind-rattling forty-minute video comparing the various I.T. blogs written by that other Haber brother, Morey, to the words of John Titor. This text comparison is dubious at best. Given the large sample sizes used by The Hoax Hunter, any two authors would be found to use an equal if not greater number of similar words. The Hoax Hunter's best evidence is that both Morey Haber and John Titor use words like *per-*

manently and *infrastructure* on a regular basis. To quote a recent YouTube comment from someone using the handle Acefireburst, "I came into this video with an open mind, but this is the least compelling evidence ever."

At one point Morey Haber did author a blog referring to his association with the John Titor story. Far from being an admission of his involvement, the blog underscored the importance of managing one's Google results. That blog has since been taken down.

The most common 'solution' to the John Titor mystery is that Richard or "John Rick" Haber authored the posts and then eventually enlisted his brother to represent the story to the public. This still doesn't answer how Richard Haber knew all that John Titor knew. Simply being in computer science does not grant a person inside knowledge regarding the engineering of the IBM 5100, or the production of the Segway, or little-known goings-on at CERN.

When asked about this by the *Where is John Titor* interviewers, Richard says, "I do have a computer background, more of an administrative or I.T. admin type position. Yes I do program, but in no way, shape or form am I involved."

Larry then adds, "The most he does is fix computers, get people's passwords and he does some basic websites."

Ultimately, the same question that applies to Larry applies to Richard: If he wrote the John Titor posts, what was the purpose? If it was for profit, where are the profits? If it was for fame, why not come forward? The only answer that adds up is that Richard Haber simply wanted to tell a good yarn. If that was his intention—mission accomplished.

Joseph Matheny

"The first requirement for any piece of writing is that it must be alive."

– F. Scott Fitzgerald quote featured on Matheny's website.

Joseph Matheny's bio reads as follows:

> Joseph Matheny is a pseudonym used by a plethora of evolutionary intelligence agents throughout the galaxy. Like Monty Cantsin, Luther Blisset or Saint Germain, you never know when or where he's going to pop up. He is rumored to never sleep, moonlight as a technology consultant, daylight as a fireproof vampire, live by the motto: Non Serviam! and almost never fail to leave a ticking time bomb behind.

What does he do, you ask?

> Joseph is a "Hypermedium" who believes that Occam's Razor is not a disposable. Joseph Matheny is a Curator, Contributor and Producer of seditious sites like Greylodge, and Alterati. Joseph seems to be a verb. Joseph Matheny is an Internet litterbug, leaving flot-

> sam and jetsam all over, to hopefully act like a message in a bottle. If you read it, you will be infected. If you are infected you will be InFicted. If you are InFicted, you will get UnFucted. Meanwhile, Joseph is holding himself hostage until all his demands are met.

Given so edgy a self-description, it's interesting to note his many accomplishments that could fill out a more credible-sounding bio. He's worked in the tech sector since 1993, was a relatively big wheel at Netscape and Adobe, and holds a number of patents. More relevant to our purposes, he is considered the primary authority behind one of the Internet's first alternate reality games, *Ong's Hat*.

It's important to understand that Matheny identifies as a culture jammer. Michael Kinsella, author of *Legend-Tripping Online: Supernatural Folklore and the Search for Ong's Hat* has referred to Matheny as an 'archetypal trickster.' Before eventually coming clean as one of its authors, Matheny gave a number of conflicting interviews that made it difficult to pin down his involvement in *Ong's Hat*, or whether or not he even perceived it as fiction.

What's certain is that *Ong's Hat* began in the early 80s on early BBS systems and in photocopied publications. It gained traction during the late 90s and, according to Kinsella, reached its peak of popularity in 2001. The good folks at *Know Your Meme* do a good job of describing it:

Though *Ong's Hat* may not have set out to be an ARG, the methods by which the author interacted with participants and used different platforms to build and spread its legend has been reflected in later games. Also known as *The Incunabula Papers*, the game incorporated the practice of "legend tripping" in which a group of people visit sites known in folklore for horrific or supernatural events. Matheny built a mythos around a supposed ghost town in New Jersey throughout the 1980s through works disguised as research shared on bulletin boards and physical zines.[...]Between 1994 and 2000, posts about *Ong's Hat* were planted on a number of different Usenet groups to spark discussion, including sci.math, alt.illuminati, alt.conspiracy and alt.society. paradigms, among others. In 2001, Matheny stopped the project and went on to publish two books about it, as well as archiving all the materials on the Incunabula website.

Adept participants would recognize veiled references to Borges and the Church of the SubGenius mixed in with flourishes of chaos science and quantum thinking. One similarity to the John Titor posts is a major plot element involving technology allowing travel to parallel worlds. Much of *Ong's Hat* is presented as a catalog of fictional, as in "made up," esoteric books. There happens to be one on time travel that shares some elements with the science involved in the John Titor story.

> 3. ibid. Faster Than Light: Superluminal Loopholes in Physics (NAL,1988) Some of the theorists who touch on the Many-Worlds "hypothesis" place too much emphasis on time distortions and the implication of "time travel". These of course seem present in the theorems, but in practice have turned out (so far) to be of little consequence. Chaos Theory places much more emphasis on the temporal directionality than most quantum theory (with such exceptions as R. Feynman and his "arrow of time"), and offers strong evidence for the past-present-future evolution that we actually experience. As K. Sohrawardi puts it, "the universe is in a state of Being, true, but that state is not static in the way suggested by the concept of 'reversibility' in Classical physics.

In a 2003 interview with *New World Disorder Magazine*, Matheny described the four people who originated the *Incunabula*, describing one as a 'poetic terrorist,' another as a physicist, and yet another as a 'media and network hacker.'

> They decided one day to take some pre-existing fiction bits, stir in some current pop science, parody of paranormal conspiracy literature and graffiti it on the walls of the noosphere. Boys will be boys after all. Over the years, others in certain academic circles

were brought in to work on updating and upgrading the concepts employed and to integrate the lesson learned into other projects, **some of which are currently underway.**

A lot of that sounds like it could apply as easily to John Titor as it could to *Ong's Hat*. It certainly seems like Joseph Matheny, that old fireproof vampire and verb, possesses all of the experience necessary, as well as the peer group, to create a tale like John Titor's.

Given all this, imagine the impact Matheny made when he appeared on *Project Archivist Episode 138* to rather dismissively take credit for the story. This may well be another act of culture jamming on Matheny's part. But then it's the only interview he's given on John Titor, so it will have to stand as Matheny's official position until he says something contradictory.

In the interview he claims to be one of four people behind the John Titor myth. *Ong's Hat* was "going strong" but Matheny was disappointed that the game was attracting conspiracy theorists rather than gamers. Matheny believes conspiracy theorists "were the worst game players in the world…no sense of humour."

While Matheny wanted his collaborators to take credit for the story with him, one said yes and the other two said no because they didn't want to hurt their careers, believing that too many crazies would come out of the woodwork to bother them.

The inner circle of the *Ong's Hat* group had recognized that time travel was a hot trope on Art Bell's *Coast to Coast AM* at the time, and they admired the creativity of some of Art's time travel callers. Matheny says he called in as Josh to a *Coast to Coast AM* episode featuring Oliver Williams.

The John Titor idea was part "proto-trolling attempt" but also to "do something and we'll never take credit for it, so that there's always this open-ended mystery that will echo through the generations.[...]Really what we wanted to do was we wanted to create a modern myth on the Internet.[...] We wanted to do one where no one could be pointed to. That was the Achilles' heel of the *Ong's Hat* thing, was that I'd used myself as a character in the story so there was always a person to point to." And so Matheny and his cohorts would send John Titor back to the future in the grand mythical tradition. He would disappear like a puff of smoke.

Matheny claims the Titor posts have different voices because different people were posing as Titor online. Matheny was hesitant to handle the postings because he didn't want to slip up, though he does take credit for putting together John's character, saying that "everyone should figure out" that John was based on *The Terminator*. "John Titor, John Connor" he says assuredly. He claims John Titor's temporal displacement unit was "just a bunch of stuff put together to look impressive" made by a professional prop builder, but his prop builder friend was no longer willing to take credit for his work.

Matheny claims his partners were up-and-comers in the media industry, working in post-production, who are no longer interested in being associated with the project. But after they "let it go" in 2001 they saw the "thing get bigger and bigger....and finally culminating with all these websites popping up."

Matheny continues to ridicule the story, saying how easy it was to generate the props, to mess with Art Bell, all while never stepping out from behind the curtain.

"If you stick the IBM 5100 in the middle of it most people will roll their eyes and know this is a put-on. I always like to have a wink and a nudge in there so the intelligent, sane person will go 'oh this is a put-on,' but I'm going to keep reading because I'm being entertained. I like to put obviously stupid things in the middle of something..."

The hosts manage to acknowledge the accurate predictions Titor did make, and attribute these to "extrapolations" made by Matheny based on his tech experience. For example: the 5100 narrative comes about as a result of Matheny's UNIX experience.

He claims to be "almost insulted" that his name doesn't come up one time in John Titor speculation. Maybe that's why he listed the project on his LinkedIn page and a link to the *Project Archivist* interview is the first clickable option on his website.

Matheny didn't mind the breakout success of the Titor story at first, but then, "It really got weird." Documentary films were made. The John Titor-focussed anime series *Steins;Gate* was produced. All of this Matheny approved of.

What bothered Matheny was Larry Haber and his involvement with the now-out-of-print *John Titor: A Time Traveler's Tale.* One of Matheny's rules for this project was not to use it for "exploitive gain." He says they didn't have copyright, but if they saw profiteering happening they'd "take the pins out from under it."

"The entertainment lawyer rubbed me the wrong way," said Matheny, who claims the book is out of print because he contacted Haber and told him in no uncertain terms "You're talking to John Titor, motherfucker" and that he'd go public with "what a fucking fraud you are."

Matheny said Haber never got back to him, but two days later the book had been pulled from sale. Again, Haber has called these claims "bogus."

In Kinsella's *Legend-Tripping Online*, he details a number of posters on *Ong's Hat/Incunabula* forums who expanded the ARG experience by bringing in arcane references to northern Californian cults or the works of British sci-fi writer Michael G. Coney. This larger phenomenon in alternate reality gaming was detailed in Dave Szulborski's *This is Not a Game*, and the (TINAG) acronym has come to define games that leap outside the bonds of their original narrative. In fact this seems to be half the fun of an ARG for some participants.

If Matheny's claims are true, then every bit of effort expended in tracking down information about Larry Haber and his brothers is just a bizarre and (arguably: fruitless) extension of the game. And Larry Haber didn't just steal Matheny's intellectual property; he made himself a character in that intellectual property.

Kinsella quotes ARG designer and gaming advocate Jane McGonigal as saying, "One of the most intriguing and lingering effects of TINAG immersion tactics is a tendency to continue seeing games where game don't exist."

The *Project Archivist* interview is frustrating because Matheny is making bold claims, earth-shattering claims to a John Titor obsessive, but the hosts seem content to cherry-pick whatever details they can snicker the most obnoxiously at. By the end of the interview I realized they hadn't asked Matheny a single hard question, had not pinned him down in any way to provide proof.

What's fascinating is that there's a perfect little piece of proof that Matheny could have provided: an *Ong's Hat* reference in the actual John Titor posts.

> **Posted by Sally Stanton on 02-12-2001 08:16 PM**
>
> *Talking*
> *Watch me pull a rabbit out of Ong's Hat!!*
> *Anway, 'scuze me. Gotta run. My kitty's*
> *looking for that Door into Sumer (sic).*

All this means on the surface is that one of the posters was a fan of *Ong's Hat*, and, also, apparently Robert Heinlein. It also lends some credence to claims made by The Hoax Hunter that some of the accounts responding to John were made up (plants) to create the impression that more people were interacting than there really were. We'll get into The Hoax Hunter in more detail later, but this always struck me as a credible theory: it solves the question of "How did John answer so quickly?" Well, because he knew the questions in advance.

As interesting as any of Matheny's claims is the relationship between Matheny and Temporal Recon, the anonymous author behind *Conviction of a Time Traveler*. The damning coincidence that links them will be revealed in the following Temporal Recon chapter.

An Interview with Joseph Matheny

Mike Sauve: If I was sceptical after the *Project Archivist* interview, I became more confident that you had some involvement with the John Titor story after seeing this in the original John Titor posts:

Posted by Sally Stanton on 02-12-2001 08:16 PM

Talking
Watch me pull a rabbit out of Ong's Hat!!
Anway, 'scuze me. Gotta run. My kitty's
looking for that Door into Sumer (sic).

Yet during the *Project Archivist* interview you said you aimed to:

> *"do something and we'll never take credit for it, so that there's always this open-ended mystery that will echo through the generations.[...]Really what we wanted to do was we wanted to create a modern myth on the Internet.[...] We wanted to do one where no one could be pointed to. That was the Achilles' heal of the Ong's Hat thing was that I'd used myself as a character in the story so there was always a person to point to."*

The two don't add up. If you don't want the Titor story to be traceable, why include this *Ong's Hat* reference?

Joseph Matheny: Easy enough answer. That wasn't one of "us." A lot of people latched onto the phenomena as it grew and with the relative anonymity of the Internet it was easy and obviously inevitable that there would be a lot of cryptic (non)-players throwing a lot of red herrings.

Mike Sauve: Alternatively, if you were looking to take credit for the Titor story in that interview, then why didn't you provide any hard proof? Part of this might be the fault of the hosts, who never pressed you, and even seemed a bit sycophantic. Still, I felt some of your claims were a bit broad and dismissive, and that if you really are behind the story, and want the credit, you could have established your authorship more definitively. Can you provide me with any hard proof that you are behind the John Titor story? I want to believe. It will make my life easier.

Joseph Matheny: You want to believe? I think I misconstrued your intentions. I assumed (my fault) that you were a serious journalist who was going to do some kind of dispassionate and objective analysis of the phenomena. As to your assumption that I was "looking to take credit for the Titor story," which I never actually said, let me make it clear: I was merely seeking to go on the record. I do not seek to take credit, because in honesty I was merely one of a few people involved. Also, it's not important to me from a resume point perspective, but rather just something I wanted to get off my chest before moving on completely from ARG/meta-fiction completely. It kind of bothered me that so many people take this story seriously and while I will not expend energy on defending anything to do with the JT project, I feel satisfied in having gone on the record, so in the future, it can never be said that I didn't. I tried, very hard to get others to go on the record, but looking at the reaction of the milieu that's grown up around the JT mythos about most revelations and/or suspicions; I cannot blame them for wanting to stay far far away from it. The Internet brings out the worst in some people.

Mike Sauve: You said that you contacted Larry Haber and told him to take *John Titor: A Time Traveler's Tale* off Amazon. He denies this ever happened. If your claims are true, then it seems strange to me that a lawyer with a credible practise would choose to risk his reputation in this way, and for what gain? If he was intending a film, and your threats stopped the film, why does he still make appearances on shows like *Fade to Black with Jimmy Church* to fan the flames?

Joseph Matheny: I didn't say "I" contacted him but rather that he was contacted. Also, let's break it down (I really shouldn't have to do this). 1.) John Titor was not a real person. 2.) An entertainment attorney put out a book about a fictional person claiming to have received the content from the family of said FICTIONAL PERSON and passed it off as real. 3.) What gain? I don't know. MONEY? He saw an exploitable market and one he thought he could exploit without fear of reprisal ("they can't speak up without blowing their cover.") and he was almost right. Your attitude towards this tells me you haven't really dealt with the marginality of the entertainment industry. Compound that already distasteful milieu with the equally grotesquery of the attorney cadre and you have what Gary Busey calls a GUT MAGGOT.

Mike Sauve: Based on the *Project Archivist* interview, I don't believe you'll reveal the identities of your alleged co-horts. But I'll ask anyway. Is Oliver Williams involved? Is Jimmy Church involved? There was a cryptic Reddit post that was quickly deleted implicating you, Oliver Williams, 'someone who worked on *Ghostbusters*,' and Bryan J. Glass, writer of *The Mice Templar*. This struck me as just odd enough to maybe have some validity. And I've always suspected Williams.

Joseph Matheny: Hahahah. Jimmy Church contacted me about...2 years ago (?) to appear on his show about JT and ARG and I think I left him butthurt because after doing some due diligence (I had never heard of him) I kinda let him have both barrels of my thinking about the "conspiracy theory crowd." So, needless to say, rule him out. As to the other people you suspect, no. Never heard of them.

Mike Sauve: The following post seems incongruent with John's others. Is this an example of one of your cohorts not being on board with the message, or someone being tired/drunk/high when they were posting, or what exactly?

Dear Fellow Time Travelers:

In about 30 days, I will be leaving this worldline to return home to 2036. I first want to say thank you for the wonderful conversation and insight into your society. I have learned a great deal and my opinion on quite a few things has changed dramatically.

I will finish the questions that have been posted on this site up to this date. Unfortunately, I must now spend my spare time preparing to leave and I will not be on the computer very much. I do however want to repeat my offer and add a slight twist.

After going over my flight plan home, I have discovered my VGL holdover period is a bit longer than I expected. I will be spending at least three weeks in April of 1998 as I make my way back to 1975. Therefore, I not only offer you the chance to leave a message to yourself in 2036 but I offer you the chance to leave yourself a message in 1998. I will take any compiled messages and email addressees you provide and send them on the net when I get to 1998.

Granted, this will not affect you on your worldline now but you make take some comfort that another you on another worldline has the advantage of knowing something you wish you knew three years ago. Based on the earlier questions Ive seen, Ive decided a day-to-day record of the Dow a day in advance should convince you that the messages are real in 1998.

In addition, I am hopeful a series of photocopies and photographs will be available for you that may give you more insight into the technology of the distortion unit. I will let you know the address of the site when it is available. I also plan to have my parents videotape my departure. If they succeed, it will also be posted after I leave.

I look forward to these last few weeks with my family and I will check in periodically to check this site.

*Live in Peace 2001,
John*

Joseph Matheny: That wasn't me. I was busy closing up shop on *Incunabula* so I wasn't always in the loop on what people did or said. I had windows of more involvement and windows of less.

Mike Sauve: Similarly the first fax to Art Bell does not really line up with the subsequent posts. Was this a proto-effort at telling the story that was later discarded? Interestingly, from the 'Titor is real' perspective it actually makes sense if it's an alternate Titor coming back with a slightly alternate mission, so if that was the intent it's rather ingenious.

Joseph Matheny: Let's call that the Beta phase. Remember, this was all new territory, so we had to try things and then adjust as time went on to tighten up what worked and discard what didn't

Mike Sauve: Though he has denied it. I've noted some significant ties between you and Temporal Recon, the author of the 'Titor is Real' manifesto *Conviction of a Time Traveler*. One of his blog posts about Titor is titled "Journey Through the Incunabula," yet the post has nothing to do with either *Ong's Hat* or 16th century pamphlets, and at the time he denied having heard of either you or *Ong's Hat*. He pleads ignorance at every turn, and also engages in a lot of double-speak that is reminiscent of John Titor's rhetorical ability to dodge questions he does not want to answer.

Joseph Matheny: Interesting theory. I think Temporal Recon is yet another opportunist and may either be giving the *Ong's Hat* material a nod or dropping it as a red herring.

Mike Sauve: The Hoax Hunter has argued that most of John's interlocutors were plants. This would answer the question, "How was John able to respond so quickly?" Well, because he knew the questions in advance. Was this the case? The Hoax Hunter has also denigrated you, incidentally, saying:

A desperate dude named Joseph Matheny claims on his LinkedIn profile and blog website that he's the "artist" behind the John Titor story. Yet magically provides zero proof backing up this claim. The dude is an artist alright, but closer to a con-artist. He's a bandwagon fan who probably heard about JT a few years ago and decided to take credit for John Titor and every modern hoax that none have come forward to take credit for. It's a nice scam but I doubt it'll make his resume look any better.

Joseph Matheny: LOL. Wow, I've been denigrated by some random guy on the Internet. Will wonders never cease. Yes, some were plants, others were not. Am I supposed to respond to some person taking a potshot at my "resume"? LOL. Next question.

Mike Sauve: *Ong's Hat* contains a lot of Everett-Wheeler content. Safe to assume you were the person behind all the Everett-Wheeler content in the Titor posts, acting as a science advisor of sorts?

Joseph Matheny: That's a safe assumption. Ok, there you have it. Hope that helps. Sorry, but this interview is concluded and I don't have anything else to say on the matter. I have nothing to defend or prove. People will believe what they want and at the very least they cannot say I didn't leave a trace of the truth out there somewhere. I have moved on and now write on academic subjects under a pen name. I never disclosed for the purpose of fame or fortune. I did so so I could walk away completely and not feel like I left a loose end unattended. I used to say to people, "I hope you find what you're looking for." but have since modified it to, "I hope you find what you're looking for was worth the effort."

Temporal Recon

"All of us are unavoidably a product of the world from whence we come. Can a time traveler be any different?"

– Temporal Recon

Temporal Recon is the pseudonym used by the anonymous author of an excellent, comprehensive book called *Conviction of a Time Traveller*. The book makes a scholarly, sometimes legal-sounding case that John Titor is most likely a real time traveller. The book also has a number of references to government overreach, as does Temporal Recon's Facebook page, creating an impression that he's a constitutionalist, just as John Titor seemed to have been.

When I first read *CoaTT*, I wondered if it was written by Larry Haber because of the legal-sounding rhetoric. Then I had a discussion with Temporal Recon on Facebook. I was surprised to find a man speaking in an altogether different tone than the author of the book. While the book is very formal and precise, the things Temporal Recon said struck me as almost new-agey. The same is true for some of his blogs and interviews. Compare this first quote from his book:

> In investigating the Titor story, I quickly came to the same realization that many before me did: 100% proof doesn't exist in this case. Subsequently, I applied the

same standard for evidence as a court of law. While we don't have eyewitness testimony of John Titor arriving on our (to use a term he coined) "wordline" from an unimpeachable witness, we do have information that he provided to use that we can now, 10 years later, intelligently assess with a little bit of intellectual honesty. Circumstantial evidence plays a commanding part in the "conviction of" of John Titor due to the fact that convincing hoaxes are rarely self-evident as being hoaxes; by definition that's what makes them exceptionally convincing.

To this one from T.R.'s blog:

As I move further and further into the Grand Portal of the larger mystery, new theories only beget new questions; questions I would not have had the perspective to ask only a few short years ago. I am finding in my continued interest in the topic that, with new information assimilated into the whole, the borders of what I thought I knew continue to be pushed yet outward. I suppose this is the manner in which understanding is gained, which can only be described as painfully slow in our desire for answers *now*. As

> I am coming to understand, this stratagem for the proliferation of information is a 'time-tested' method and appears to have been around a very long time. I am forced to question now, *"How much more could there possibly be?"*

On first glance, this does not hold particular relevance. It's entirely possible that T.R. chose to write *Conviction* in the most formal tone possible so that sceptical readers would take it more seriously. Surely the best aspect of *CoaTT* is its rigorous dismantling of the debunkers' more dubious arguments.

There is also a possibility that the person presenting himself as Temporal Recon is not the author of *Conviction of a Time Traveler* at all. And that since no one else has come forward to take credit he's free to use the book to create a platform for his own anonymous persona. That strikes me as unlikely however.

And then there's the Joseph Matheny coincidences. During a podcast interview T.R. was asked if he was familiar with Matheny's alternate-reality narrative, *Ong's Hat*. T.R. said he was not familiar with Matheny, but T.R. had previously confirmed on Facebook that he 'might go' to a Joseph Matheny interview, suggesting, although not concretely, that he was at least vaguely aware of him.

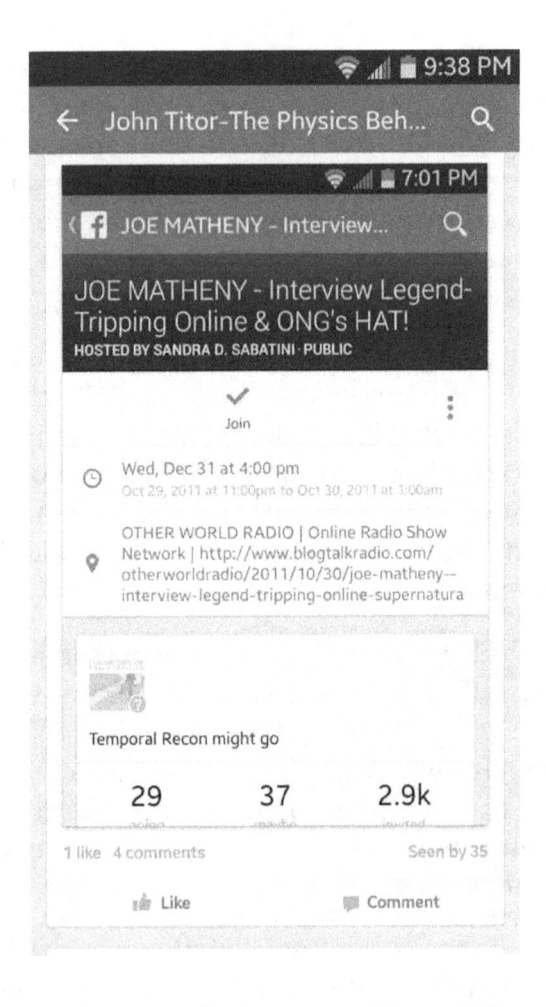

That's not all that earth-shattering. T.R. could have been friends with the organizer of the event, or the interviewer, and maybe the Matheny connection is accidental.

But consider this more alarming coincidence. What became Matheny's *Ong's Hat* was initially titled *The Incunabula Papers.* A May 10, 2014 post about John

Titor on T.R.'s website was titled *Journey Through the Incunabula*.

> In my interactions with the general public over the years, I have come across many people with varying levels of interest in the John Titor posts. Some of those people are wholly wedded to their conclusions and assumptions as they pertain to the John Titor story. As a result of this steadfast assuredness, new (and seemingly contradictory) information finds little purchase. It withers on the ground in spite of the perfect viability to explain an aspect of the larger picture. In spite of my and others' best efforts to toss the idea over the high wall of the ego, the wall remains and the new idea is deflected and rejected.

Incunabula is defined as "a book, pamphlet or other document that was printed, and not handwritten, before the start of the 16th century in Europe." Temporal Recon's essay focuses on how people reach their respective conclusions about John Titor. There are no references to 16th century pamphlets. And there's no real rationale for the use of *Incunabula* in the title. How else to interpret the presence of this obscure word other than as a wink at Matheny?

I asked Temporal Recon if he was affiliated with Matheny and he denied it, saying, "As for explaining the glaring parallel, I cannot. Sometimes, the universe is just damn mysterious. As I said, I was as surprised to see it [the *Incunabula* coincidence with Matheny] as you were. Unfortunately for you, your position does not afford you the certainty that I have that it really is just a very strange coincidence. Albeit, a coincidence that has my full attention at the moment. I'm just as curious about it as you are, but for different reasons."

Temporal Recon is very good at diverting a conversation away from subjects he doesn't want to discuss. And you better believe the Matheny connection is not something he wants to discuss. In fact, Temporal Recon's facility with side-stepping unwanted questions bares a striking resemblance to John Titor's same ability.

In a separate, more formal interview, I asked him again about the Matheny coincidence and he responded with his typically mind-rattling double-speak.

> Well, a good place to start might be to establish what evidence you would accept one way or the other. What does a Matheny-TR tie look like? What does a false Matheny-TR tie (i.e. a coincidence) look like? Would you be able to tell the difference? Is there any difference between the two?
>
> As for that blog post, I find no need to defend myself against anything. If there is a tie between Matheny and myself, and I am

unaware of it, well, we are talking about time travel, aren't we? Perhaps I'm simply not aware of the tie yet and you are simply ahead of me on making that connection.

Alternatively, if there is a tie between Matheny and myself, and I AM aware of it, I see little reason to admit to it here/now.

There is, of course, a third alternative, but I'll leave that for you to explore (consider it a nudge)."

In a later conversation he doubled back and said "*Ong's Hat*...does connect to the larger context." But then refused to expand on this statement, saying, "It would be akin to describing a single bolt on a freight train," and later acting as though he had very little knowledge of what *Ong's Hat* or an alternate-reality game even was.

Keeping with the ARG theory, if Temporal Recon was a co-hort of Matheny's, then both *CoaTT* and its forthcoming sequel are doing more than any game player or participant other than perhaps Larry Haber to keep the story alive and pulsing. And yet Temporal Recon has little patience for any suggestion that the John Titor story is anything but established fact.

In dealing with Temporal Recon, I could never be entirely sure if he was leading me down the primrose path. He will make cryptic statements that allude to hard evidence he's accumulated that proves the existence of multiple time travelers not named John Titor currently on our world line. But when pressed, he clams up, or remains coy. It can be frustrating, but also kind of fun trying to extract information from T.R.

What his book does so well is defend the evidence that Titor is indeed a time traveller against the evidence that someone wrote the story, and time and again he reaches the conclusion that for a non-time traveler to have written the account, they would have had access to a great deal of privileged information, been knowledgeable in several high-end fields of study, and been incredibly intelligent to maintain the rouse in real time on chat sites. Could it be that Temporal Recon is one of the authors of the John Titor story, and that's why he's not only able to, but motivated to, defend the story's strong points so vehemently?

On August 23, 2016 he announced a sequel to *Conviction of a Time Traveler* that "will take more the form of a memoir of my background, experiences and the many things I learned along the way concerning the 'time travel' question. Ultimately, this book will be a no holds barred exposition of *everything* I know and think I know about our favorite topic. The reason for this memoir is to document my understanding of the question for my posterity and to create a record of that understanding that will last as a family heirloom well into the future."

He also posted the Table of Contents for this sequel. Its highlights include a list of known time travelers, the revelation that T.R. has a remote viewing background, and that he, like Marlin Pohlman, has filed or at least written a time-travel related patent. I believe it's worth re-printing here in full, because if T.R. delivers on what this TOC promises with anywhere near the level of rigour that went into *CoaTT*, it may well prove that John Titor was a time traveler, rendering this current book irrelevant, nothing more than a historical oddity to be studied with gleeful disdain when they open the John Titor wings of various universities.

Conviction of a Time Traveler II

Provisional Table of Contents

1. Acknowledgements

2. Preface

- Why COATT II?

- Who is this book for?

- Who is this book *not* for?

3. Introduction – Who is Temporal Recon?

- My Personality

    - Of Dinosaurs and Fifth-Graders

- Why I choose to remain anonymous

- How I chose the *Nomme de Guerre* "Temporal Recon"

- My Background and my unique insight into the Question
  - My work in West Africa and other parts of the world
  - Remote Viewing and the Monroe Institute
- Thoughts on Consciousness
- Thoughts on the ET

4. What Started It All

- My rediscovery of the John Titor story
- The JT story in a nutshell – A Synopsis
- "The Sandbox" – What is it?
- Selected findings from COATT I
  - The Evidence
  - Missing Predictions
- COATT I response by fans, debunkers and others
  - Sales and Opinions
  - Unique Attention
- Selected Conclusions from COATT I

5. "The Education of Temporal Recon"

- Online Status Quo: Stuck on Stupid

- Cutting My Own Path
    - Heurism

6. Updates to Findings from COATT I

- Failed Predictions were only a surprise to those who don't understand

- Multiple World Interpretation – A mission requirement not a constraint

- The Fax Enigma, Analysis & Conclusions

- The "Secret Song" identified

- Discussion on temperatures

- Examples of Missing and/or Corrupted Posts

- The Real Purpose for "A Time Traveler's Tale"

7. Down the Rabbit Hole

- Who is?:
    - "Oliver Williams?"
    - "Pamela Moore?"
    - Art Bell
- Research into other claimants
    - The Florida Nexus
    - The Post Office Story

- Application of the 'INT – Establishing Time Traveler Techniques, Tactics & Procedures
- How to Identify a Time Traveler
    - Of Yardsticks & Signposts
- The Time Travelers and Affiliates
    - The Categories of Time Travel Claimants
    - General profile
    - What is an Affiliate?
    - List of identified Known and Suspected TT'ers or Affiliates
- Command and Control relationships
    - Time Traveler Organization Chart
    - Mapping TT'ers across time
    - A Timeless Iceberg – Observations and Conclusions from Analysis of the Map
- Breaking The "Code" – Analysis, its use and implications
- The Technology
    - The laughable patent troll, Marlin Pohlman, PhD
    - How to extract electrical energy from a black hole, its ties to the "177" Patch and my patent

- The Gravity Engine, how it really works and further discussion on my patent
- The Pen Laser photograph and why it is legitimate
- Technology Constraints
  - Celestial constraints, considerations and implications – Sol-Lunar Impact
  - Time and Location
- Physical trace evidence
  - Examples of Physical Trace Evidence
  - Notable Years and their implications
  - Notable locations and their implications
- Multiple World Theory and Divergence
  - Analysis and implications of what MWT really means
  - Divergent vs Convergent
- The Variable Gravity Lock – Not what we were told
- Calculating Divergence – A How to Guide

8. Unanswered Questions (Doing the Debunkers' job for them)

- Where are the Tracks?

- Of atomic clocks and footlockers
- Measuring Gravity
- TBD
- Conclusion

9. Discussion on Time Travel Missions

- Mission Scope
- The constraint of hamegin
- Mission Tradecraft
    - Cut outs and backstops
    - Dead drops
    - Pseudonym use
    - Web Proxies/anonymization
    - Safe Houses
    - "Affiliates"
- Communication methods and examples
- Mission Constraints

10. The Philosophy of Time Travel

- Balancing the sovereign right of choice with mission goals

11. Other Time Travel Programs and Groups

• The Implications

12. Adversarial Elements

• What do I mean by "Adversarial Elements?"

• Why do I call them "AE?"

• Evidence for AE's presence

• Evidence of "Controlled Operations" online

13. Overlap into Other topics

• Consciousness

• The TT/ET connection

  • Technological

  • Qualitative

• Acknowledging a much larger context

14. Who is really calling the shots?

• The WM'ers

• WM techniques and examples

15. Bringing It All Together

• The (Very) Big Picture and its effect on my outlook

16. Selected Essays

- Purpose of the essays
- Selected Essays

Let us close this chapter on Mr. Recon with a piece of advice he gave me, "Curiosity and objective observation can lead to very interesting conclusions. If you truly want to understand the truth, your first step must be to discard the conventional wisdom surrounding the Titor story and strike out on your own; start from scratch. It's worth it."

An Interview with Temporal Recon

Mike Sauve: You talked about physical traces left in our environment by John's time travel unit, and that these might be traceable in order to confirm the story. Why aren't more people talking about this?

Temporal Recon: Simply stated, because the majority of people who are interested in the Timetravel_0 story, even those who say they "believe," in all actuality, do *not* believe it. Because they do not "believe," they never break free of the Timetravel_0 narrative which results in their never considering it in *real* terms and what that would mean.

Once one can fully accept the topic as real, one is then released from the Timetravel_0 narrative and free to explore its implications, in all their forms.

Mike Sauve: This was posted on the *Time Travel Institute* by someone claiming to have seen a time traveler arrive in 2005. How valid would you say this claim is:

> I had actually witnessed—in late July of 2005—the event while it was happening. The only thing I'm selling is my testimony to the validity of time travel: Having already occurred on this world line; is still occurring; and in all probability will occur again

in our near future. John Titor's insignia is an actual illustrative representation of the event itself if you were to observe it while it was happening. Those outlines of concentric circles are actually present and visibly distinctive within a shimmering/rippling distortion that fans outward from a central source hugging the earth. These concentric circles are being generated at a rate of one per second. They form and progress in size and influence, moving outward—like inflating a two dimensional outline of a balloon—reaching a height where they would appear as becoming very heavy then collapsing over and falling back to earth at a slight angle, avoiding the earth bound source.

Temporal Recon: I don't typically comment on whether a poster is or isn't legit, for a variety of reasons.

Mike Sauve: You often allude to evidence regarding Titor's claims that isn't widely known. Your rationale for not disseminating this evidence seems to be that 'if people didn't believe *CoaTT*, then why would they believe anything?' It's true that some wouldn't believe. But maybe others would. If you had a piece of evidence that could prove without a doubt that one or more time travelers exist on our world line, would you publicize that information or keep it quiet?

Temporal Recon: Don't put words in my mouth that I did not state, Mike. Because I am aware of my (very) minor celebrity and that there are rumors swirling around my identity, I am exceedingly specific in the words I choose and jealously guard them.

To your question, the reason I do not simply provide what I may or may not know, or proclaim my own understanding of the TT question in general is, is simply because the information would not be *valued.* Any information that I might provide, most people would consider it opinion or speculation and dismissed in favor of their own well-guarded preconceptions.

As a result of this very human and normal reaction to new or discordant information, I have opted to simply provide nudges. Trust me, it may be a slower road to truth, but once reached, it is impervious to the slings and arrows of those stuck in the quicksand of Conventional Wisdom.

There are other reasons of course, but I feel the above answers your question, mostly.

Mike Sauve: Outside of reaching out to Paula at Microsingularity.net for a recent interview, your handle also appears in a number of other publications. The author of a *Pacific Standard Mag* article quotes you as saying,

> "ONE OF THE KEYS to cracking the Titor question," starts an email by someone who goes by the name Temporal Recon, "is to just allow for the possibility that time travel very well *could* be true."

Why do you reach out to these people? Are you John Titor's PR man?

Temporal Recon: I reached out to Paula because she and I have a long standing and ongoing (yet sporadic) conversation which is partly comprised of those nudges I spoke to you about. Her interest in the topic is legitimate and I wish to foster her interest towards the larger truth. In regards to my most recent interview with her, I felt the need to discuss a few topics, so I availed myself to her questions and thus made myself available to her.

As for the other excerpt you provided, I do believe I remember that particular interview. The author wished to write an article on the John Titor story and its adherents. I imagine my name came up when he googled the story and so he reached out to me with his questions as someone with an abiding interest in the topic.

From the tone of his questions, it became obvious to me that his interest was *not* necessarily legitimate and was rather in search of a person of whom he could proffer as a "crazy true believer."

Truth be told, I was a bit disappointed in this and the necessity to assume a mildly adversarial stance with him. Because I couched my answers with that understanding in mind, I left him no room to mock. As a result, all he was left with was the small quote he provided. My answers were worded in such a fashion as to checkmate him away from his intent to selectively edit my responses into something that could be held up as 'crazy.' As a result, all he was left with was the small quote he provided.

His resulting article was proof positive that I had correctly read his intent and handled him appropriately. As insurance, I published my full responses on my blog. I'm sure they are still there if you care to search it out.

So to answer your question, other than Paula, I reach out to nobody. Why bother? If I have something to say, I have a blog. Absent that, another book is always a possibility as well, is it not? I'm not lacking for an ability to express myself.

You did make me chuckle here at the idea that I might be on JT's payroll. Quite the well-oiled machine you are implying: an entertainment lawyer, A PR agent AND a by-name domain presence? Not bad, though I would say he might not be getting his money's worth out of me since I rarely post.

Mike Sauve: This may be an impertinent question, but I'm curious to know how *CoaTT* is doing, how much feedback you receive, etc.

Temporal Recon: Only mildly impertinent. All the comments I receive are readily seen on the Amazon site. As for comments sent to me privately, well, those are private, aren't they?

Mike Sauve: The Matheny question has to be asked. Joseph Matheny has publicly claimed to be one of four authors behind the John Titor story. While his claims on the *Project Archivist* podcast seem overblown, and the hosts never really press him for proof, there is an *Ong's Hat* reference in the original John Titor posts. Similarly, you titled a blog of your own about John Titor "Journey through the Incunabula." *Incunabula* is defined as "a book, pamphlet or other document that was printed, and not handwritten, before the start of the 16th century in Europe." That's not what your post was about. This seems too glaring to be coincidence. Can you defend yourself against the presumption that you are either in league with Joseph Matheny or Matheny himself?

Temporal Recon: Well, a good place to start might be to establish what evidence you would accept one way or the other. What does a Matheny-TR tie look like? What does a false Matheny-TR tie (i.e. a coincidence) look like? Would you be able to tell the difference? Is there any difference between the two?

As for that blog post, I find no need to defend myself against anything. If there is a tie between Matheny and myself, and I am unaware of it, well, we are talking about time travel, aren't we? Perhaps I'm simply not aware of the tie *yet* and you are simply ahead of me on making that connection.

Alternatively, if there is a tie between Matheny and myself, and I AM aware of it, I see little reason to admit to it here/now.

There is, of course, a third alternative, but I'll leave that for you to explore (consider it a nudge).

Oliver Williams

"It's disturbing to read something you want to believe that has so many negative aspects to it. To stay sane, you have to find a reason to discount it."

– Oliver Williams

Every time I hear Oliver Williams speak, I get a strong intuition that he is behind the John Titor story in some way. It's not just how knowledgeable he is of even the most minute details; anyone could obsess over the story until they have an encyclopaedic knowledge of it. What gets me is that Oliver Williams describes the John Titor story exactly like an author would describe the contents of his book.

Williams claims that he became involved with John Titor lore in 2001 when a friend sent him links to the original posts. Williams then spent several sleepless nights immersing himself in the *Time Travel Institute* and *Post to Post* content, eventually leading him to create JohnTitor.com on May 23rd, 2003.

Williams discussed his initial interest in Titor during an interview with Tim Ventura.

> After staying up all night reading, I was amazed and continued to follow the posts. One of the statements John made was that his time machine was powered by two

mini-black holes that were manufactured in a particle accelerator called CERN in Geneva Switzerland. He made the statement in his posts that CERN would announce their expectations to create mini-black holes in the fall of 2001. Amazingly, that's exactly what happened six months after he left. That feeling of 'oh my gosh' stuck with me. I think it's the main reason people keep following the posts.

As time went on, more and more of what John said about our future began to unfold and there were more 'oh my gosh' moments. You would read the posts and forget them until you saw something in the news that reminded you that a time traveler spoke about it a year ago. That's what prompted me to collect the actual words John wrote online and put them into one spot that was easier to read.

Despite its outdated design, dead links, and no real updates in years, JohnTitor.com is still a top hit for a John Titor Google search, and was receiving 10,000 hits a day as of 2013. Williams has stated that a large percentage of the site's traffic comes from NSA, CIA, and U.S. Air Force web addresses.

The site's lack of maintenance seems to abdicate Williams of responsibility. If he's behind the John Titor legend, why go to so much effort only to let a key landing place for every new John Titor enthusiast waste away?

The Hoax Hunter believes Williams isn't invested because he wrote the story, but because he's profiting from John Titor merchandise. "What makes him guilty is his advertisement (sic) for the official John Titor Foundation café-press site that sells official John Titor foundation mugs, t-shirts and bumper stickers. Oliver makes no money from clicks to this store, he either made a deal with the John Titor Foundation or is best friends with them, or he is the official John Titor Foundation webmaster. My nickname for Oliver is For-Sale-Oliver. Since he's the number one expert on JT merchandise."

On January 3rd 2014 Jimmy Church interviewed Larry Haber for a John Titor special. It was the first Titor news in some time, although Haber didn't have much to say, only promising some news in the next few months. News that never manifested, incidentally. Moments after Haber hung up, Oliver Williams phoned in unscheduled to the open lines portion of the show.

As he'd done on several *Coast to Coast* interviews, Williams again established himself as the clearest, most confident voice when detailing the John Titor narrative. Jimmy Church is one of the best-informed media personalities on the subject, but still Williams consistently one-upped him in terms of recalling specific details.

Highlights of that interview include:

When Church says that Haber is aloof, and may need to be as a lawyer, Williams responds incredulously, "Why does he agree to go on your show? Why do that? It makes no sense."

He says, "Larry and I had contact once about 3-4 years ago. It was because of those guys that were making the videos. [*Where is John Titor*] They were trying to reach me, or I got a hold of them. Larry and I had a brief contact by email and that was it."

"When we first started doing this we got death threats." It's curious that he would use the *we* pronoun. He's never mentioned having any kind of partner on JohnTitor.com. He has spoken of the death threats several times.

Williams reveals for the first time that he lives in Leesburg, Florida. Another Florida connection. He claims the Florida connection made the story interesting for him in the first place because he knew the landmarks referenced by Titor.

At one point, Church says, "I've never spoken to you before. Everyone needs to understand...this truly came out of the blue." If this interview was an act, Williams was better at pulling it off than Church was.

When Church brings up Titor not warning about 9/11, Williams reminds Jimmy Church of the 1998 Art Bell fax that mentions skyscrapers missing in

New York. Much like an author who doesn't want a key aspect of his work ignored or misunderstood.

Williams says, "Whoever did this they knew how to draw, they knew about physics, they knew about the IBM computer. They were able to read and analyze the news well enough that they could make predictions a couple months in the future that were pretty much correct. And they had the ability to write. So either that was one single person that was on the Internet for three months and decided to make no money doing this or it was 6-7 people..."

When Church tells a story about getting a Skype call from one of the Joint Chiefs of Staff after he'd announced an upcoming John Titor show, Williams is beyond incredulous. He sounds like he's barely disguising outright disdain in his voice when he says that he can't let himself believe claims of this nature.

Maybe this isn't enough to accuse Oliver Williams of 'selling the story.' But he does have a tendency to gloss over important distinctions that call for skepticism, preferring to present only the best evidence in detail.

THE BIT PLAYERS

Pre-Existing Influences

> *"...The struggle was not against a human enemy, or for victory. The struggle, for those who survived "The Day", was to survive the next."*
>
> *– Pat Frank, "Alas, Babylon"*

Over the years observers have noted that some aspects of the John Titor story seem to have been influenced by pre-existing texts or cultural phenomena.

The most glaring example of this might be that John Titor's time machine was conveyed in a 1967 Corvette. Of course the most famous time travelling car of them all was the DeLorean used in *Back to the Future*. This seems almost too 'on the nose' however, and throughout his posts John gives plausible explanations for why a car is the ideal conveyance for his temporal displacement unit.

> **Pamela**: by the way can you tell me what it feels like to time travel' when you are in the process of doing it what does it feel like and what do you see and hear. you made mention that you had to get use to the fields. Do you see a bright flash of light'
>
> **Timetravel_0**: Interesting first question. The unit has a ramp up time after the des-

tination coordinates are fed into the computers. An audible alarm and a small light start a short countdown at which point you should be secured in a seat. The gravity field generated by the unit overtakes you very quickly. You feel a tug toward the unit similar to rising quickly in an elevator and it continues to rise based on the power setting the unit is working under. At 100% power, the constant pull of gravity can be as high as 2 Gs or more depending on how close you are to the unit. There are no serious side effects but I try to avoid eating before a flight. No bright flash of light is seen. Outside, the vehicle appears to accelerate as the light is bent around it. We have to wear sunglasses or close our eyes as this happens due to a short burst of ultraviolet radiation. Personally I think it looks like your driving under a rainbow. After that, it appears to fade to black and remains totally black until the unit is turned off. **We are advised to keep the windows closed as a great deal of heat builds up outside the car. The gravity field also traps a small air pocket around the car that acts as your only O2 supply unless you bring compressed air with you.** This pocket will only last for a short period and a carbon sensor tells us when it's too dangerous. The C204 unit is accurate from 50 to 60 years a jump and travels at about 10 years an hour at 100% power. You do hear a slight hum as the unit operates and when the power changes or the unit turns off. There is a great deal of electrical crackling noise from static electricity.

Pamela: 2.What is the dimension of the field around the car? How many feet out from the car would you say it goes?

Timetravel_0: It can be adjusted to some degree. The CG (center of gravity) is adjustable within about 4 feet and the unit is effective about 10 to 12 feet in either direction from there. The vertical distance is quite a bit shorter and is determined by sensors in the unit.

Pamela: 6.how hot would you say the temperature gets on the outside of the car while in operation?

Timetravel_0: Very! hot. Depending on the power setting, 100 to 120 degrees is average.

Pamela: 7.is the car in drive mode when the device is activated or is it totally turned off?

Timetravel_0: The car is off and the brake on.

While the *Back to the Future* connection may be minimal, the John Titor story does bare a stronger connection to another work of fiction, Pat Frank's post-apocalyptic classic *Alas, Babylon*.

Originally published in 1959 during the height of cold war concerns about nuclear obliteration, its jacket copy reads as follows:

> "Alas, Babylon." Those fateful words heralded the end. When a nuclear holocaust ravages the United States, a thousand years of civilization are stripped away overnight, and tens of millions of people are killed instantly. But for one small town in Florida, miraculously spared, the struggle is just beginning, as men and women of all backgrounds join together to confront the darkness.

Let's note the similarities. Both *Alas, Babylon* and the John Titor story are set in Florida. *Alas, Babylon* refers to the day of the nuclear event as *H Day* while the John Titor story refers to the date of the event as *N Day*.

Both stories involve individuals banding together regionally to solve food and energy concerns once the power grid is no longer operational. Randy Bragg, the protagonist of *Alas, Babylon,* lives on a citrus farm, and is one of the first people to understand the importance of sharing resources with his community. He is also responsible for inspiring his friends to launch a seagoing vessel in search of a nearby beach that is rich with salt that can be used for preservation.

Posted by John Titor on 05-01-2001 1:46 PM

The family work we did was picking, sorting and shipping oranges by sailboat up and down the coast of Florida. We were expected to produce a certain amount for the community and a certain amount for other communities as agreed to by our CLC. In exchange, we received power, water, a certain amount of food and other necessities that were produced inside our community.

We've discussed the concept of John Titor authors as role-players, but might the story have taken inspiration from an existing role-playing game? A May 13, 2016 article by Rick Schwartz for *Stranger Dimensions* points out some eerie similarities between Titor's posts and a *Dungeons & Dragons*-like game called *GURPS Cyberworld*. More specifically, Schwartz points to a variant on the game's setting posted by a user called Spearweasel in the early 90s.

Here are some of the similarities between the game's narrative and the John Titor story according to Schwartz:

2004 – Resentment festers until it hits a peak in 2004, as "militia movements" begin to rise and challenge the Provisional Government. Chaos ensues. Martial law is declared, and the U.S. Constitution is suspended.

2005 – A new United States Civil War effectively begins in Idaho and Oregon, leading to the deaths of 2,000,000 U.S. Citizens.

2015 – The Second Civil War ends in 2007, and a new Reconstruction begins. This doesn't last, as the Cold War heats up with a "Russo-Japanese Coalition." The United States finds itself on China's side. In 2014, Russia and Japan launch a "single massive attack," hitting China, Alaska, and Europe with "small atomic weapons." This leads to retaliation, and the Third, and presumably very short, World War begins."

While the dates and actions don't line up exactly, there is some broad overlap, especially regarding U.S. Civil War around 2004 and a devastating nuclear attack in 2015.

Posted by John Titor on 02-01-2001 08:36 AM

The year 2008 was a general date by which time everyone will realize the world they thought they were living in was over. The civil war in the United States will start in 2004. I would describe it as having a Waco type event every month that steadily gets worse. The conflict will consume everyone in the US by 2012 and end in 2015 with a very short WWIII.

The militia movements that played into Spearweasel's campaign were a big part of life throughout the 90s. Ruby Ridge, Waco, and the Oklahoma City bombing were all fresh in people's minds. Recall that the world was in a state of relative stability in the years prior to 9/11 and one of the foremost issues on American minds was this festering conflict between the U.S. federal government and people like Timothy McVeigh who considered himself a "Constitutional Defender."

In this case, what may have influenced the author(s) of the John Titor story wasn't a cultural artefact, but actual stories ripped from the headlines. Time and again John spoke of a need to understand the U.S. constitution, of the right to bare arms, and of being wary of government overreach.

Posted by John Titor on 21-11-2000 21 at 10:41 PM

While you sit by and watch your Constitution being torn away from you, you willfully eat poisoned food, buy manufactured products no one needs and turn an uncaring eye away from millions of people suffering and dying all around you.

Posted by John Titor on 26-11-2000 4:32 PM

Do not eat or use products from any animal that is fed and eats parts of its own dead.

Do not kiss or have intimate relations with anyone you do not know.

Learn basic sanitation and water purification.

Be comfortable around firearms. Learn to shoot and clean a gun.

Get a good first aid kit and learn to use it.

Find 5 people within 100 miles that you trust with your life and stay in contact with them.

Get a copy of the US Constitution and read it.

Eat less.

Get a bicycle and two sets of spare tires. Ride it 10 miles a week.

Consider what you would bring with you if you had to leave your home in 10 min. and never return.

Posted by John Titor on 26-1-2001 1:32 PM

After the war, the United States had split into five separate regions based on the various factors and military objectives they each had. There was a great deal of anger directed toward the Federal government and a revival of states rights was becoming paramount. However, in their attempt to create an economic form of government, the political and military leaders at the time decided to hold one last Constitutional Congress in order to present a psychological cohesion from the old system. During this Congress, the leaders discovered and decided that coming up with a new and better form of government was nearly impossible. The original Constitution itself was not the problem it was the ignorance of the people that lived under it.

Art Bell

The John Titor story would never have reached the popularity it has without Art Bell. Assuming it is a work of fiction, the story may never have been written at all if it weren't for the late night radio legend.

That's because in the 90s the hottest spot for time travel discussion was Art Bell's *Coast to Coast AM* radio show. It was also the hottest spot for discussion of UFOs, electronic voice phenomenon, reverse speech, Area 51 callers, Coming Global Superstorms, and that nasty old Harlot the Witch. The best feature of Art's golden age *Coast* episodes was his penchant for letting the open lines breathe. If he got a credible-sounding caller, he'd often keep that caller on the line for several segments.

This not only introduced the world to modern classics of Forteana such as "Mel's Hole." But also a number of alleged time travelers.

Like In 1997, when Signal Seven, the 'paleo-ag-tech' from 2063 'got rid of his homing device' and eluded his 'travel time group' to tell Art that in the future they're "trying to change the weather." Signal Seven claimed he was sent back to find "the earlier cousins of corn, wheat, tomatoes, and things that can survive in a hotter temperature. We'll use them to splice and make hybrids in the future."

Over time, Art would even have specific open lines for time travelers. The results ranged from hilarious to vaguely plausible. One 1997 caller claimed to be from 2063. When Art was repeating the man's story he said "If you are from the year 2036..." The caller then corrects Art, and Art says, "Trying to catch you there." While 2036 is a near-inversion of 2063, some people believe this was an early reference to John Titor by Art.

Beyond these contributions, Art's *Post to Post* message board was one of the two primary means of communication for John Titor. John Titor started posting on *The Time Travel Institute* message board on November 2, 2000, and then migrated to *Post to Post* on January 27, 2001, introducing himself with this now infamous post that is often erroneously described as John Titor's first post.

Posted by John Titor on 01-27-2001 12:45 PM

Greetings. I am a time traveler from the year 2036. I am on my way home after getting an IBM 5100 computer system from the year 1975.

My "time" machine is a stationary mass, temporal displacement unit manufactured by General Electric. The unit is powered by two, top-spin, dual-positive singularities that produce a standard, off-set Tipler sinusoid.

I will be happy to post pictures of the unit.

However, it's possible Art Bell was being contacted by John Titor several years prior to that post. Art was the conduit for a bizarre false start in the John Titor story. This first fax was sent in 1997, and obviously contains several aspects of the John Titor story, including references to CERN, changes to the constitution and the evolution of a 'communal government.' It also contains several aspects that don't align with the John Titor story, such as Y2K not occurring. Titor truthers have speculated that this may be because John Titor actually returned to 1998 to prevent Y2K.

When leaving 2001, John said he had to return to 1975 to retrace his steps in order to return as close as possible to his original 2036 world line. Along the way he planned on stopping in 1998.

Posted by John Titor on 03-10-2001 07:26 PM

After going over my flight plan home, I have discovered my VGL holdover period is a bit longer than I expected. I will be spending at least three weeks in April of 1998 as I make my way back to 1975. Therefore, I not only offer you the chance to leave a message to yourself in 2036 but I offer you the chance to leave yourself a message in 1998. I will take any compiled messages and email addressees you provide and send them on the net when I get to 1998.

Is the following fax simply an alternate John saying alternate things because they really are different for him? Or is it, as Joseph Matheny has suggested, "a trial run." If that's the case. It's one more brilliant aspect to the game. The authors had the foresight to send this fax in 1998, only to reference John Titor returning to 1998 while he was posting in 2001.

The First Fax to Art Bell – Read on *Coast to Coast AM* on July 29, 1998

"Dear Art,

I had to fax when I heard other time travelers calling in from any time past the year 2500 AD. Please let me explain.

Time travel was invented in 2034. Offshoots of certain successful fusion reactor research allowed scientists at CERN to produce the world's first contained singularity engine. The basic design involves rotating singularities inside a magnetic field. By altering the speed and direction of rotation, you can travel both forward and backward in time.

Time itself can be understood in terms of connected lines. When you go back in time, you travel on your original timeline. When you turn your singularity engine off, a new timeline is created, due to the fact that you and your time machine are now there. In other words, a new universe is created.

To get back to your original line, you must travel a split second father back, and immediately throw the engine into forward without turning it off.

Some interesting outcomes of this are:

One, you meet yourself. I have done it often, even taken a younger version of myself along for a few rides before returning myself to the new timeline and going back to mine.

Two, you can alter history in the new universe that you have just created. Most of the time, the changes are subtle. Sometimes, I'll notice car models that don't exist, or books that come out late.

The oldest one was a skyscraper that wasn't built in a near favorite store of mine in New York.

Interestingly, when you travel in time, you must compensate for the orbit of the earth. Since the time machine doesn't move, you have to adjust the engines so you remain on the planet when you turn it off. Unfortunately, it was also discovered that anyone going forward in time, from my 2036, hit a brick wall in the year 2564.

Everyone who has ever been there has reported that nothing exists. When the machine is turned off, you find yourself surrounded by blackness and silence.

Now, most time travelers are trying to find out where the line went bad by going into the past, creating a new universe, and proceeding forward to see if the same thing results in 2564. It appears the line went bad around the year 2000. I'm here now, in this time, to test a few theories of mine before going forward.

Now, for the future you might want to know about.

One, Y2K is a disaster. Many people die on the highways when they freeze to death trying to get to warmer weather.

Two, the government tries to keep power by instituting marshall law, but all of it collapses when their efforts to bring the power back up fail.

Three, a power facility in Denver is able to restart itself, but is mobbed by hundreds of thousands of people and destroyed. This convinces most that maybe we shouldn't bring the old system back up.

Four, a few years later, communal government system is developed, after the constitution takes a few twists.

China retakes Taiwan, Israel wins the largest battle for their life, and Russia is covered in nuclear snow from their collapsed reactors.

Art, the reason I'm here now is because I believe a nuclear weapon set off by Iraq in the Middle East war with Israel might have something to do with the damaged timeline. I will test that theory and get back to you.

Please pray that we discover the reason why there is no apparent future after 2564."

The eeriest aspect of this first message, sent in 1998, is the reference to the "missing skyscraper."

A second fax sent later in 1998 was John's first reference to having pictures of his time travel unit. It is also more consistent with the details of John's story that would emerge in the new millennium.

The Second Fax to Art Bell

"Dear Mr. Bell,

I am glad you're back. I faxed this information to you the day before you left the air. I wanted to make sure it wasn't lost in the shuffle so I am sending a gift. If you've already seen this please accept my apologies. If you choose to make this public please do not publish the fax number. I had to fax when I heard the other time traveler calling in from the recent time past in fact the year 2500 Ad.

Let me explain, Mr. Bell. I sent a fax with this opening on July 29 1998. As I said then I am a time traveler. I have been on this world line since April of this year and I plan to leave soon. Typically time travelers do not purposely affect the world lines they visit. However, this mission is unusually long and I've grown attached to some of the people I have met here.

Anyway, for my own reasons I have decided to help this world line by sharing information about the future with a few people in the hope that it will help their future. I am contacting you for the same reason. Unfortunately there is no historical reference to your program in my worldline.

I believe you can change your future by creating one now.

Some of the information presented on your program may be invaluable to up-line researchers. I suggest you isolate the programs that concentrate on military technology and new physics theories. Transcribe these programs and put them someplace safe away from the box. I recommend someplace in the midwest.

I also urge you to reconsider your paranoia to the Russians.

They are not preparing for war with the average US citizen. They are preparing for war with the US government. They will eventually save this country and the lives of million of Americans.

I realize my claims are a bit difficult to accept so I will send the following once I know you have received this fax. A few pages from the operations manual of my time machine. And a few colored photographs of my vehicle.

If you wish to contact me I will be happy to share with you the nature of time, the physics of time travel and some of the events of your future.

Please send a return package to…"

Pamela

"Timetraveler_0~
When it is beginning to rain....
it is time to go rainbow gazing."

– Pamela Moore

No poster interacted with John Titor as frequently or as intimately as Pamela Moore. In addition to being one of the most frequent posters in both the *Time Travel Institute* and *Post to Post* threads, she also interacted with John over instant messenger (although never over the phone) and claims to have shared a deep bond with John.

Beyond this, Pamela also claimed that John Titor provided her with a "secret song" that could be used to verify anyone who'd come forward claiming to be John Titor. Most significantly, she claims that John Titor mailed her a piece of the IBM 5100 logo, and that while it came with no return address, there was an Orlando postmark.

Since the days of the original posts, Pamela has become reticent to take part in interviews or interact with John Titor aficionados.

In 2009 she did open up in an interview with The Hoax Hunter, saying

> First of all the label from the IBM. It is not necessarily the label from the IBM he went after. He asked me what I would like from him and I told him I wanted something that traveled

through the blackhole with him even if it was a small piece of paper. He chose to send me this label. It was never meant to prove John was a time traveler. He never mentioned that it came from the computer he was suppose [sic] to get. It was simply an item that went through the blackhole with him. That's it. And if this was true then the very label itself was made up of atoms from another worldline. Back then that was very exciting to me.

She mentions having given a small piece of the label to Phil Fiord, a fellow John Titor follower. In 2015 Fiord decided to sell the item through a third-party seller for $10,000 on eBay. It remains unsold. Here is the listing:

If you are familiar with John Titor, you may be aware that he mailed Pamela Moore the label from the back of the IBM 5100 as a proof. They had become more personally close. After Titors' departure, Phil Fiord flew to an agreed location and met with Pamela Moore. She gifted him with this cut from the actual label. As it was a gift and is a treasured item by him, he is loathe to sell it, but he has decided it is something that many have expressed interest in having for research purposes. He hopes this may go to someone who may be able to further explore and maybe advance the truth behind Titor.

Prior to enlisting my aid to sell this, Mr. Fiord had been in contact with Rick Donaldson from the same era of discussion as well as Olav, the admin and owner of Anomalies.net.

Message me if you need more information, but please respect that I am acting as a selling agent for Mr. Fiord only.

One frequent source of intrigue is an alleged John Titor departure video. Larry Haber has claimed that this exists and that Kay Titor is in possession of it. Pamela tells The Hoax Hunter, "I never did receive John's departure video. Even after receiving a letter from John's 'mother.' I had contact and constantly asked where the video was and never received an answer."

Pamela goes on to detail why she is not wholly trusting of Larry Haber and the potentially fictitious Kay Titor. "I really don't know if he is representing anyone real or not. I have no proof either way. All I know is that a letter was forwarded through the foundation from the mother to me. That's the person who is supposed to be Larry's client."

She confirms that the John Titor Foundation was never able to confirm the secret song, but does provide the JTF with an out, suggesting maybe John Titor never mentioned the secret song to anyone but her, since the song came up in a chat that no one may have had access to.

"He said he was going to tell his mother," said Pamela, "However, whoever was posing as his mother did confirm some things in a letter to me to at least tell me that she had access to his emails. When I got a copy of the book [*John Titor: A Time Traveler's Tale*] it was signed and at the end there was a quoted song. However it was not the song that John told me to remember."

Pamela is a respected, if elusive, figure in the John Titor community because even after being as involved as anyone with the story, she has remained fair-minded and skeptical. As she told The Hoax Hunter, "John never proved to me he was a time traveler. However he did know things other people didn't know. He never hesitated to tell you either... even in chats. He would say 'hold on a minute...' next thing you know you were looking at knowledge no one else had at the time."

Pamela now accepts The Hoax Hunter's finding that the P.O. box once registered to the John Titor foundation was previously registered to John R. Haber, thus implicating Richard Haber as an author. Despite her acceptance of the Richard Haber hypothesis, Pamela may still be a key figure in unraveling this entire mystery. As she says, "I have to be careful with what I say. A few things I must keep secret so if John ever decides to come forth I will have info to confirm it was the same John who posted as John Titor."

Hoax Hunter

"To the diehard Titor fans, probably nothing will convince them even if Haber admitted to being Titor."

– The Hoax Hunter

Most of what needs to be said about The Hoax Hunter has already come out in previous entries regarding the Haber brothers, Pamela, and Joseph Matheny. Take this as testament to the quality and comprehensiveness of his detective work. The one video in which he strums his guitar and sings a diss track aimed at Matheny is amusing in a cringe-worthy way, but troll tactics like these may prevent some from granting The Hoax Hunter's findings the credence they deserve.

His foremost contribution was discovering that P.O. box 47071 was registered to John R. Haber before it was registered to Larry Haber. No one, including Larry, can offer a credible explanation for this. For many this is the final nail in the coffin.

The Hoax Hunter also did some comprehensive, no doubt gruelling work in tracking down all the names involved in the Titor posts, and coming to the conclusion that 88 of those names are fakes.

"The closer you look at these names, the more they look like they were quickly made up," writes The

Hoax Hunter in a Feb 13, 2009 post, "If they were the names or pseudonyms of real people they would have likely talked about Titor somewhere else on the net using their posting name whether they believed in the hoax or not due to its widespread fame. According to Google they all vanished when Titor vanished."

In this same post he isolates the non-suspects, and finds there may have been as little as thirteen actual 'non-plants' interacting with John Titor.

Like many once involved heavily in the John Titor debates, The Hoax Hunter seems to have stepped back into the shadows. Just as Temporal Recon feels about his diametrically opposed conclusions, The Hoax Hunter believes he has proven his point to an unassailable extent, and that any further efforts to convince people are a waste of time.

Steven Gibbs

"This device is so simple to build you probably won't believe it."

– Steven Gibbs

One of the definite 'real people' mentioned in the original John Titor posts was Kansas resident Steven Gibbs. He has appeared several times on *Coast to Coast AM* to discuss (and try to sell) his own time travel technology, the Hyper Dimensional Resonator. He also claims to have sold one of these HDRs to the adult John Titor. Unfortunately the HDR doesn't seem to rely on any real technology, but rather a lot of astral plane-related baloney. If after the machine is bought and paid for, after you've hooked it up to your stomach chakra, then if your consciousness still isn't sent back in time, Gibbs has a simple explanation—Why, you aren't close enough to a vortex!

Anyone who's ever heard his *Coast* appearances may well reach the same conclusion as The Hoax Hunter:

> Quite frankly after hearing Gibbs on *Coast to Coast AM* various times, if not every time, he does not sound smart enough to be behind the words of John Titor. He peddles electric boxes (HDR) 'Hyper-dimensional Resonator' units as time machines but isn't well versed enough to be a convincing Ti-

tor, he may have played a part but I doubt it. After the Titor story was broadcast on *Coast to Coast AM* Gibbs claimed he met Titor but he claims a lot of things.

According to his bio, "Steve Gibbs was adopted by the Gibbs family who raised him on a farm near Clearwater, NE. Although never fond of school, Steve finished high school and took trade school courses in electronics. He gained an excellent reputation for fixing things, putting things together, and installing things while helping the family farm. Steve has devised a machine that he claims will allow the user to actually travel through time."

In 1981 Gibbs claims he was visited by another Steven Gibbs, or sometimes it's by two aliens, and either this future Gibbs or these aliens had a diagram for a machine he was then calling a Sonic Resonator. Author and academic Jason Offut describes using the machine in a *Mysterious Universe* blog:

> The Hyper Dimensional Resonator is a small box with dials, ports for the "time coil" and 'electromagnet,' and three small switches. To program it for time travel, dial in the day, month and year desired, although there are only two dials and they both go to 10. I haven't figured that one out. The directions were confusing, and a bit frightening. Typed in all caps on a typewriter, the directions indicate that as the user I must put a quartz crystal and some of my DNA into a hole called a "witness well"

(spit, hair, but not blood. The instructions say blood brings demons), wrap a coiled electric cord around my head, place a strong electromagnet between my legs, and rub a finger on a flat plate on the front of the machine.

Even after exposing his brain and genitals to a good deal of electromagnetic energy, Offut failed to achieve time travel.

There are testimonials from HDR users claiming that strange things occurred after using the machine. Patricia Griffin Ress, who authored a book on Gibbs, claims that after using the machine, dialogue in one of her favourite movies, *Shane,* had somehow changed on her. This calls to mind the recent *Berenst*in Bears* or Mandela Effect phenomena. However, Ress' *Stranger than Fiction: The True Time Travel Adventures* is little more than a hodgepodge of typos, religious zealotry and pseudo-scientific overreaches.

Ress gives Gibbs free-reign in her book to expound on the scientific underpinnings of the HDR. However, they are more concisely presented on Gibbs' website HDRUsers.com. A few highlights:

> "Most of this technology is old Philadelphia Experiment technology."

> "According to Steven Gibbs you must be over a grid point magnetic vortex in order to time travel."

> "A vortex is a dimensional doorway often an area of strange paranormal events such as ghosts and UFOs being sighted."
>
> "I can detect a vortex by using an EMF detector. These EMF detectors are used by ghost hunters and other people interested in paranormal phenomena." "The HDR uses the vortex which is a magnetic anomaly to punch a hole to the other realm."

Despite the dubious nature of all this, Steven Gibbs does have some minor place in John Titor lore, as his name does come up twice in the original John Titor posts. There's a pretty rational explanation for this: the same kind of person who'd interact with a time traveler on a message board might also be willing to fork over a few dollars for a HDR.

Posted by John Tooker on 02-02-2001 02:21 AM

Hey,

You're a traveller too? Have you ever interacted with any of the pre 1983 staff, at Montauk? If so, you may have met me. When I was working there, I was a R&D assistant to Dr. Von Neumann, and was known as Daniel John Waters, and had a rank of Lt. Col., in the Psi Corps. BTW, this isn't my original timeline, as I believe that I jumped timelines, not long after doing some work with Steve Gibbs, on his trip up to Calgary, Canada.

John

Posted by E. Robert Gonzalez on 03-04-2001 03:35 PM

Question. I have been a temporal researcher for at least two years now and mostly studied radionic forms of time travel. I personally have not yet used one of the devices but have heard stories and evidence leading me to think they work. I was also wondering if you have heard of any of the radionic and Steven Gibbs devices.

Marlin Pohlman

"Are you saying that John Titor came back in time to drug and assault women?"

– Above Top Secret message board poster 'Lampsalot'

Now we come to the interesting and ultimately tragic case of Marlin Pohlman. In 2011 Pohlman shocked the John Titor community by applying for a patent based on schematics and drawings from the GE Manufacturer's Manual that Titor posted. The initial assumption was that Pohlman had to be some kind of crank. If he wasn't, it would have wide-reaching implications, including that A) Titor's alleged technology was legitimate enough to go through the patent process, and B) Marlin Pohlman may either be an author of the John Titor story or have strong connections to its authors.

The crank analysis was soon weakened by Pohlman's bona fides. He had the starchy title of Director of Governance, Risk and Compliance Product Strategy for a reputable software company. He'd also authored three textbooks. His text *Oracle Identity Management* is described on Amazon:

> Dr. Pohlman examines multinational regulations and delves into the nature of governance, risk, and compliance. He also cites common standards, illustrating a number

of well-known compliance frameworks. He then focuses on specific software components that will enable secure business operations. To complete the picture, he discusses elements of the Oracle architecture, which permit reporting essential to the regulatory compliance process, and the vaulting solutions and data hubs, which collect, enforce, and store policy information.

A little dry? For certain. The domain of the crank? Most certainly not.

Then there is the superficial verisimilitude of the patent itself. It is thirty pages of material that is well above my pay-grade in terms of scientific understanding. But it certainly looks like the legitimate work of a PhD calibre mind. To get a taste here is the abstract:

> A method for employing sinusoidal oscillations of electrical bombardment on the surface of one Kerr type singularity in close proximity to a second Kerr type singularity in such a method to take advantage of the Lense-Thirring effect, to simulate the effect of two point masses on nearly radial orbits in a 2+1 dimensional anti-de Sitter space resulting in creation of circular timelike geodesics conforming to the van Stockum under the Van Den Broeck modification of the Alcubierre geometry (Van Den Broeck 1999) per-

mitting topology change from one spacelike boundary to the other in accordance with Geroch's theorem (Geroch 1967) which results in a method for the formation of Godel-type geodesically complete spacetime envelopes complete with closed timelike curves.

Sinusoidal oscillations do sound legit. However, the patent could never be approved, because the technological underpinnings remain theoretical, as they do not yet exist.

All of the diagrams included in Pohlman's patent are lifted directly from Titor's posts. Isn't it the good plagiarist's first rule to at least make a few superficial changes, and not just lift the JPEG off the Anomalies. net message board?

As alluded to above, the Marlin Pohlman saga ends on a troublesome note. On October 13th 2013, Pohlman, then 43, pleaded guilty to attempted second-degree assault, unlawful possession of ecstasy and unlawful possession of the drug ketamine after he'd been accused of drugging and abusing women.

Maxine Bernstein, a court reporter for *The Oregonian,* describes Pohlman's crimes:

> The attempted assault charges stems from an incident last December when he enticed a woman at a party he had once dated to his car to inhale nitrous oxide, laughing gas. While

> Pohlman and his former girlfriend were in the back seat of the car, she said he injected her in the neck with a drug using a spring-loaded medical syringe. She was hospitalized and unconscious for at least four hours.
>
> A physician found concentrations of the drug Scopolamine in the woman's system, which can be legally obtained and often is used to treat nausea. But prosecutors have said the drug is infamously used by Colombian gangs to block memory.

These distasteful revelations were more than enough to quell any Pohlman-is-Titor discussion on the various websites where the Titor legend lives on. Pohlman could now be written off as a drug-crazed loon; moreover, a dangerous and immoral person.

But it's worth noting that Pohlman's alleged drug-of-choice, ecstasy, is not a psychedelic drug; it's not even a drug like meth that cuts a clear path towards psychosis. Nor is it even a physically addictive drug, per se. The other drug he was caught with was ketamine, a cat tranquilizer popular in rave scenes for its trippy effects and the amplification of ecstasy's potency. Ketamine's loopy sensation wears off in a matter of minutes, if not seconds.

Ecstasy is usually some combination of MDMA, a smallish amount of amphetamine or some lower-end stimulant, and depending on the scruples of the supplier, a whole host of other potentially hazardous components. It is remotely possible that the ecstasy Pohlman was taking had enough amphetamine in it to lead him into the realm of mild amphetamine psychosis. It's more likely that the drug served as a trigger for existing mental health issues Pohlman was predisposed towards.

What strikes me as the most probable connection between Pohlman's ecstasy use and his authorship of the Titor-inspired patent is one of the foremost trademarks of the ecstatic experience: grandiosity.

It's interesting to consider the patent as Pohlman's pet ecstasy project. With each tab did he become wild-eyed and sit down to once again "invent time travel?" We can look at the apparent rigour of the patent as evidence that it was produced by a relatively clear mind, but if Pohlman had a high level of education, even jacked up on E, he would still be able to clearly articulate himself in that type of language.

There are humanizing posts from Pohlman himself on *Above Top Secret*. Including one in which he discusses his five-year battle with cancer and empathizes with another poster whose father was going through the same chemotherapy treatment Pohlman did.

> **marlinpohlman:** I had a great deal of time during Chemo, four years and Oracle did not let me do any IT related work so the patent was my pet project sitting on the beige couch with the IV

Drugs were good, weight gain was bad, short-term disability pays the bills but puts your career back a couple of years. Had two cute caregivers who lived with me but was too sick to make a move. Sense of smell goes up 200% which is not always good.

I am in Silicon Valley trying to float a company based on my ex-wife's patent and the ISO27017 Cloud Control Standard (I am editor) for that purpose. I will make the device or die trying but only a billionaire or a multinational can pull this off. If someone dropped cash in my lap or hired me to build it I would do it in a heartbeat no question.

I have spoken to "Titor"'s Pamela as well as several other people related to the Time Travel legend (e.g Basiago) none of who I know personally. I am not "Titor" as Pamela will attest (we had a voice conversation and she confirmed I was not him) just a former cancer patient with a physics degree who needed something to focus on. I have worked out what to watch for and how to interfere/stop anyone using a device based on the time displacement patent... If you think one is operational near you feel free to email me marlin_pohlman@yahoo.com. I expect a few crazes but that's life.

Yes, Mr. Pohlman, imprisoned as you now are for heinous crimes, perhaps a little too motivated towards time travel for your own good, life does seem to involve a few crazies once you delve too deep into the legend of John Titor.

CONCLUSION

*And don't speak too soon
For the wheel's still in spin
And there's no tellin' who
That it's namin'*

– Bob Dylan, "The Times They Are A-Changin'"

Occasionally I bounce ideas off of Temporal Recon on Facebook. I chide him about being cryptic. He zings me for playing it safe and not committing to whether the John Titor story is real or fictional. In this conclusion T.R. will find I'm playing it safer than ever. Because if John Titor is a fictional entity, then I'm still not prepared to say concretely who is behind the story, but would prefer to split my conclusion in half.

I believe it is equally probable that Larry Haber and his brother are behind the story as it is that Joseph Matheny and his co-horts are behind the story. The two parties would seem to be mutually exclusive, given that Joseph Matheny has called Larry Haber a gut maggot, and that Larry Haber has dismissed Matheny as a non-credible figure. If the John Titor story is an alternate-reality game, however, then it's entirely possible that denigrating Larry Haber would be just one more facet of Joseph Matheny's role-playing.

If Joseph Matheny is the principle architect then there are three possibilities:

> Scenario 1: Matheny and his three friends wrote the story, Larry Haber then tried to profit from it, and Matheny called him out.
>
> Scenario 2: Matheny and co. wrote the story, hired Haber, and then called him out on the *Project Archivist* podcast to add a layer of depth to the game.
>
> Scenario 3: Matheny and co. wrote the story, hired Haber through a third-party, and Haber had never heard of Matheny until Matheny started calling him a gut maggot.

It is beyond dispute that Larry Haber is a key figure in this story. What can't be ascertained is if:

> Scenario 1: Larry Haber has opportunistically made himself a key player when he had nothing to do with the original posts.
>
> Scenario 2: Larry Haber became a key figure at the behest of his brother Richard, who may have authored the story.

Scenario 3: Larry Haber is simply a figurehead employed by Joseph Matheny, or some as-yet-unknown author of the John Titor story.

Scenario 4: John Titor is real. Kay Titor is real. Everything Larry Haber has said is 100% factual.

I thought that taking a thorough look at all the evidence would eliminate Scenario 4. But I have come across so much tantalizing evidence to the contrary that I am more inclined towards hedging than ever.

While many of these 'Titor-is-real' indicators don't fit within the parameters of this book, one compelling example is the alter-vu phenomenon that some of the original posters report experiencing. John had proposed an experiment, offering in 2001 to send 'letters' to any interested posters when he returned briefly to 1998. Pamela handled the administrative duties, collecting the messages and handing them over to John.

Posted by John Titor on 03-10-2001 07:26 PM

I offer you the chance to leave yourself a message in 1998. I will take any compiled messages and email addressees you provide and send them on the net when I get to 1998.

> Granted, this will not affect you on your worldline now but you make take some comfort that another "you" on another worldline has the advantage of knowing something you wish you knew three years ago. Based on the earlier questions I've seen, I've decided a day-to-day record of the Dow a day in advance should convince you that the messages are real in 1998.

While they don't recall receiving the letters, several of the posters/subjects report experiencing frequent alter-vus. An alter-vu might be roughly defined as memories from a parallel universe. One caller to *Coast to Coast AM* describes driving by an empty lot day after day, and then one day it is no longer an empty lot, one day it has a fully functional Walgreens operating on it. Are these individuals among the fake posters or plants that The Hoax Hunter described? Are they suffering from *folie-a-culte,* a collective delusion? Are they really experiencing alter-vus? These questions are just more ripples left in the wake of the John Titor posts.

It's aspects of the John Titor story like these that keep interest high in 2016. So much so that an obvious imposter calling himself John Titor has recently made appearances on *Coast to Coast* and *Midnight In the Desert.* The man has little knowledge of the original John Titor posts, and even has the temerity to call the original John Titor the imposter. All this individual seems to have done is co-opted the John Titor name for his own reasons. He sells hats and t-shirts. He isn't given a platform because of his credibility, but out of a hunger for John Titor content that is going unfulfilled. If you're reading, Larry, and you have those departure videos, there's no time like the present to give the world a peek. Unless a better time would be the future. I suppose the past might also be an option.

Even if this book is quickly invalidated, either by Temporal Recon, a splashy return from John Titor, or (most 'rationally') hard proof as to who's behind the story, I won't regret the effort of composition. Not only did the book refresh and fortify my knowledge concerning one of my favourite subjects of interest, but it introduced me to satisfying books like *Ong's Hat: Journey Through the Incunabula*; *Legend-Tripping Online: Supernatural Folklore and the Search for Ong's Hat*; and *Alas, Babylon*.

And so, *Tempus edax redrum*, I guess. It's been fun. John Titor, if you're reading this, send my 2001 self an email and tell him to get started a little earlier on this book.

Mike Sauve has written non-fiction for *The National Post* and *Variety*. His fiction has appeared in *McSweeney's* and many other publications. His novels *The Wraith of Skrellman* and *The Apocalypse of Lloyd* are available from Montag Press.

CPSIA information can be obtained
at www.ICGtesting.com
Printed in the USA
LVHW080901041120
670669LV00005B/751

9 781537 400839